ROMANCE MONOGRAPHS, INC.

Number 30

A THEMATIC ANALYSIS OF MME. D'AULNOY'S
CONTES DE FEES

ROMANCE MONOGRAPHS, INC.

Number 30

A THEMATIC ANALYSIS OF MME. D'AULNOY'S *CONTES DE FEES*

BY

JANE TUCKER MITCHELL

UNIVERSITY, MISSISSIPPI

ROMANCE MONOGRAPHS, INC.

1 9 7 8

IMPRESO EN ESPAÑA

PRINTED IN SPAIN

I.S.B.N. 84-399-8448-0

DEPÓSITO LEGAL: V. 1.705 - 1978

ARTES GRÁFICAS SOLER, S. A. - JÁVEA, 28 - VALENCIA (8) - 1978

Library of Congress Cataloging in Publication Data

Mitchell, Jane Tucker, 1931-
    A thematic analysis of Mme. d'Aulnoy's Contes de fées.

    (Romance monographs; 30)
    English or French.
    Bibliography: p.

    1. Aulnoy, Marie Catherine Jumelle de Berneville, comtesse d', d. 1705.
Contes de fées. 2. Aulnoy, Marie Catherine Jumelle de Berneville, comtesse
d', d. 1705 — Criticism and interpretation. I. Title.

PQ1711.A85A6535   843'.4   78-6947

To Hassie, who made it all possible.

Publication of this book was aided by a grant from the Research Council
of the University of North Carolina at Greensboro

TABLE OF CONTENTS

Page

INTRODUCTION

THE WISDOM of the fairy tale lends itself to many interpretations that run the gamut from a simple, literal explanation on the child's level to the complex, archetypal analysis of a Freud or a Jung. Scholars have broached it from every angle trying to discover its origin, its proper audience and its true significance. These and other problems relating to the fairy tale are discussed under Historical Background in Chapter I. One of the objectives of the present work is to study the modes of analyzing the fairy tale (Chapter II) and to employ those that will enhance the understanding and appreciation of Mme. d'Aulnoy's *Contes des fées.*[1]

Since the primary focus will be on the tales themselves, they will be treated thematically, that is, with emphasis on the text and on textual proof for the conclusions reached. Three characteristics of Mme. d'Aulnoy's *contes* are obvious from the first reading: her inclusion of contemporary manners which we have labeled as *Zeitgeist* and discussed in Chapter III; her love of animals and especially of metamorphoses (Chapter IV); and her treatment of love in all of its manifestations (Chapter V). Her themes are derived from tradition but are treated with variety and originality.

Finally, we have examined her style and her humor (Chapter VI) in order to show that traits such as her animal vocabulary, her irony and her use of figurative speech serve to blend the content and the form into a harmonious work full of charm and depth. In her choice of subject, Mme. d'Aulnoy is baroque in the sense of imaginative. In her choice of structure, she is classical in the sense

---

[1] Note the distinction between the title of Mme. d'Aulnoy's work, *Contes des fées,* and the genre *contes de fées.*

of logical or reasonable. We conclude, then, that the fairy tale, as developed by Mme. d'Aulnoy, is a genre that offers a perfect union of reason and imagination, of *bon sens* and *goût* as attained in the best seventeenth-century French works.

There will be no chapter on Madame d'Aulnoy's life as the emphasis here is on the work rather than the author. For details about her life and works we refer the reader to the chronological résumé of her life in Appendix I of this study and to the listings by Jal and Foulché-Delbosc in the bibliography.

The *Contes des fées* is generally considered to be the work for which Mme. d'Aulnoy is best known. That she would have preferred to be remembered for her novels or her *Relation du voyage d'Espagne* is not surprising, for the *conte de fées* was a mere pastime in the seventeenth century, not to be mentioned along with serious literature. What caused her to publish her *contes de fées* is uncertain. It may have been the success that Charles Perrault enjoyed for his *Histoires du temps passé* or it may simply have been the vogue for the tales in the French salons at the end of the century. Mme. d'Aulnoy is reputed to have been as gifted a *raconteuse* as she was a writer. Although Perrault's collection reached the public ahead of Mme. d'Aulnoy's in 1697, she does merit the title of innovator of the fairy tale since she published the first one in her novel, *Hypolite, Comte de Duglas,* in 1690, the same year she began her literary career.

Chapter I

HISTORICAL BACKGROUND OF THE FAIRY TALE

THE FAIRY TALE has finally come of age as a genre. It has been recognized as suitable adult fare and, at the same time, it has received the respect and treatment it deserves as serious literature. As recently as November, 1972, an article appeared in the *Saturday Review* which commented on the fact that children today are demanding more realism in their reading matter while adults are fleeing into worlds of fantasy.[1] Both, according to author Merla, are searching for answers to the problems of existence. The young hope to find facts that will help them cope with their environment while the adults look for deeper archetypal clues which enable them to change society. This may explain the universal appeal of the fairy tale from its inception in late seventeenth-century France to its apotheosis in this twentieth-century world.

While fairy tales have been enjoyed by children and adults through the ages, their acceptance has not always been without some apologies and considerable criticism. One of the main criticisms has centered around the audience for whom the tales were intended. If they were indeed written for children, they should be of educative value. While Perrault's tales, the first recorded ones, had an appended moral verse and were ostensibly written for children,[2] those oral *contes de fées* which preceded his in the salons

---

[1] Patrick Merla, " 'What is Real?' Asked the Rabbit One Day," *Saturday Review — The Arts*, November, 1972, pp. 43-50.

[2] However, it is interesting to note that Sainte-Beuve added that "Perrault, tout en contant pour les enfants, sait bien que ces enfants seront demain ou après-demain des rationalistes ... ," quoted in Charles Deulin, *Les Contes de*

and at the court of Louis XIV were designed for adults. In fact, aside from Perrault, most of the other French authors of fairy tales were women of the salons — Mme. d'Aulnoy, Mlle. Lhéritier, Mme. de Murat, Mme. Dunoyer and Mlle. de La Force — who had been involved in the telling of tales long before Perrault (or Pierre Darmancour) actually set his down on paper in 1697. Mary Elizabeth Storer commented that "Déjà en 1677, les dames de la Cour s'amusaient à des contes de fées qui duraient une heure." [3] According to Storer, the interest of the great lords and ladies in dressing themselves up as satyrs, nymphs or fauns for their gala affairs was an indication that they had a great penchant for the *merveilleux* and also for fairy tales because "On vivait des contes de fées avant d'en raconter." [4] Whether or not the scholars of seventeenth-century France would admit them as serious literature suitable for adult audiences, fairy tales were very much in vogue. Boileau could bemoan the lack of *vraisemblance* in such works; the Abbé de Villiers could endeavor to disenchant his contemporaries from such *mauvaise marchandise*; [5] the Abbé de Bellegarde [6] could become alarmed about the public's passion for what he termed *balivernes*; and other critics could deplore the enthusiasm for these *rêveries enfantines*; still the craze for the *contes de fées* persisted and continued in favor into the eighteenth century despite the fact that "En 1688, elles furent, par décret authentique, bannies à perpétuité de la littérature sérieuse." [7] The fact that Fénelon approved of them and used them in his instruction as preceptor to the young Duke of Burgundy no doubt contributed toward establishing a place for

---

ma mère l'oye avant Perrault (Genève: Slatkine Reprints, 1969), Introduction, p. 28.

[3] Mary Elizabeth Storer, *Un Episode littéraire de la fin du XVIIe siècle — La Mode des contes de fées* (1685-1700), Vol. XLVIII of *Bibliothèque de la Revue de Littérature Comparée,* ed. by F. Baldensperger and P. Hazard (Paris: Librairie Ancienne Honoré Champion, 1928), p. 13.

[4] Storer, p. 12.

[5] Cited in P. V. Delaporte, *Du Merveilleux dans la littérature française sous le règne de Louis XIV* (Genève: Slatkine Reprints, 1968), p. 72. Villiers, according to Delaporte, does offer some rules for the *contes de fées* in his *Lettres curieuses.* He says that the fairy tales should be sermons which teach children that virtue is sooner or later rewarded. They should have no connection with religion and they should imitate the simple style of the nurses who related them (pp. 95-96).

[6] Delaporte, p. 73.

[7] Delaporte, p. 68.

them in modern literature. In any case, their publication was wel-comed by the public well into the next century as witnessed by the appearance in 1785 of the forty-one volume compilation of the *Cabinet des fées*. Deulin commented on the attitude of the eighteenth century toward the tales when he wrote that "il y eut animadversion; aux yeux des philosophes le merveilleux encourageait les erreurs dont ils voulaient débarasser l'humanité."[8]

It is thought that after the Revolution there was little interest shown in fairy tales. However, Pierre Brochon wrote in *Le Livre de colportage* that ". . . la Bibliothèque Nationale possède près de 150 éditions de colportage des *Contes de Madame d'Aulnoy*, toutes de la première moitié du XIXe siècle, ce qui confirme la grande vogue des contes de fées dans la littérature de colportage est surtout postérieure à la Révolution."[9] The nineteenth century had its proponents of the *merveilleux* among the literati. George Sand, Charles Nodier and all of the Romantics were advocates of anything which Boileau had discredited including fairy dances and black sabbaths side by side. Prior to the nineteenth century there had been no direct communication between the intellectuals and the folk. Then, between the Franco-Prussian War and the outbreak of the First World War, the French folklore movement suddenly flowered, with the quickening of interest in philology, archaeology and ethnography.[10] Since then the scholarly work of the folklorists has added to the understanding and appreciation of folk literature, hence of fairy tales. Their work has contributed to our knowledge of the origin of some of the tales and has aided in classifying them by motifs and themes. Their methods of exploring folk literature will be discussed in a later chapter on approaches to analyzing fairy tales.

While it may seem that this discussion has wandered far afield from the initial position of the fairy tale as a genre appropriate for all ages, it has simply taken a look at what has occurred over

---

[8] Deulin, p. 29.

[9] Pierre Brochon, *Le Livre de colportage en France depuis le XVIe siècle* (Paris: Librairie Gründ, 1954), p. 84.

[10] *Folktales of France*, ed. by Geneviève Massignon (Chicago: University of Chicago Press, 1968), p. vii. (For the fascinating account of the polemic over the "Dîner de ma mère l'oye," and the formation of the French folklore movement, see Richard M. Dorson's foreword, pp. x-xliv.)

two and a half centuries to enable it to be recognized as a genre and as worthwhile adult reading. The twentieth-century critics and scholars approach their studies with a humanistic world view so that they see in the fairy tale all the symbols, archetypes and beliefs of universal man. So it is that new findings in folklore and tradition are now shared by scholars all over the world. Many modern critics agree with the article by Merla, cited at the beginning of this chapter, stating that adults like fantasy and children prefer more realism. J. R. R. Tolkien asserted that "The history of fairy stories is probably more complex than the physical history of the human race, and as complex as the history of human language." [11] Is it any wonder that many children do not like them and many adults do?

Another point of debate has been the origin of fairy tales. There are as many points of view as there are interested folklore specialists. The four possible origins most often mentioned are the Mythological, the Oriental, the Anthropological and the Ethnological. These names are not the ones always found in the discussions of the origins, but they are used here arbitrarily as the terminology which most nearly suits the theory. For example, the Mythological premise is that fairy tales are simply myths, either of elements of nature such as the Sun, Dawn, and Thunder, or of gods and heroes. Its chief exponents were Max Müller, the Grimms and even Anatole France. Max Müller is called a Solar mythologist while Anatole France falls under the rubric of a primitive mythologist. In *Le Livre de mon ami,* France explained his theory by saying that

> ... il faut penser que les combinaisons de l'esprit humain, à son enfance, sont partout les mêmes, que les mêmes spectacles ont produit les mêmes impressions dans toutes les têtes primitives, et que les hommes, également sujets à la faim, à l'amour et à la peur, ayant tout le ciel sur leur tête et la terre sous nature et de la destinée, imaginé les mêmes petits drames.
>
> Les contes de nourrice n'étaient pas moins, à leur origine, qu'une représentation de la vie et des choses, propre à satisfaire des êtres très naïfs. Cette représentation se fit

---

[11] J. R. R. Tolkien, *Tree and Leaf* (Boston: Houghton Mifflin, 1965), p. 20.

probablement d'une manière peu différente dans le cerveau des hommes blancs, dans celui des hommes jaunes et dans celui des hommes noirs. [12]

Lang referred to this belief that popular stories were the detritus of Aryan myths as the Aryan theory and he called the Oriental theory after the German Orientalist who first presented it in 1859 — the Benfey theory. [13] Others who espoused this theory that the majority of popular stories were from India and were carried all over the world were Gaston Paris as well as the three giants of French folklore at the turn of this century — Emmanuel Cosquin, Henri Gaidoz and Paul Sébillot.

Andrew Lang promulgated the Anthropological theory that there were survivals of savage ideas in popular fiction among all peoples. This view must have some rapport with Jung's archetypes, but nowhere does one find this confirmed. The evidence would indicate that the survivals of primitive ideas and the archetypes have certain commonalities. Both are symbolic and deal with inner confrontation and realizations linked with some sort of collective spirit. There is a mystical aura pervading archetypes in that they are on a high plain above the human level. In the Anthropological view of a survival of primitive ideas, there is the same yearning for something previously existing. Both claim universality. Lang stated that "... the supernatural *stuff* — metamorphosis, equally of man, beasts and things, magic and the like — *is* universal." [14] Later, Marc Soriano, who came to the psychoanalytical interpretation of Perrault's *Contes* only after exhausting all other approaches, stated that the documents gathered by folklorists showed

> ...une certaine pérennité du merveilleux, une ressemblance indéniable entre des versions recueillies à des époques et en des lieux différents. La notion d'archétype constitue en quelque sorte un passage à la limite, une généralisation de cette remarque empirique. [15]

---

[12] Anatole France, *Le Livre de mon ami*, ed. by J. Heywood Thomas (Oxford: Blackwell, 1957), p. 49.

[13] Andrew Lang, *Myth, Ritual and Religion*, Vol. II (New York: Longman's, Green, 1906), *passim*, pp. 310-30.

[14] Tolkien, p. 334.

[15] Marc Soriano, *Les Contes de Perrault, culture savante et traditions populaires* (Paris: Editions Gallimard, 1968), p. 466.

The Psychoanalytical approach to fairy tales offers a system of analysis rather than an origin of the genre or a credence in the fairy faith.

The last theory of origin was the Ethnological propounded by Joseph Bédier. In *Les Fabliaux* he gave the death blow to the Oriental theory by denying the possibility of tracing any but ethnic folktales. For him, the *fabliaux* were of French provenance. There was also a related belief in a Pygmy theory which advanced the hypothesis that belief in fairies harked back to a folk memory in some small pre-Celtic races. Another similar explanation of the fairy creatures was the Druid theory which stated that the fairies were only folk memories of Druidesses. Both of these explanations were less widely accepted than the others mentioned above.

It would be an oversight to omit the Alchemical or Mystical theory of spiritual beings existing in nature which were comparable to fairies. Each element was supposedly inhabited — the air by Sylphs, the earth by Gnomes, the water by Undines and the fire by Salamanders. The medieval metaphysicians couched their occultism in alchemical terms in order to protect themselves from persecution. Yet in the seventeenth century Montfaucon de Villars [16] used these same Elementals to attack the supernatural in Christianity in order to express his faith in a new *merveilleux* that was reasonable and fanciful at the same time. The importance of Villars' work to this study was made clear in the introductory comments by Roger Laufer when he stated that

> ... la féerie est aussi la science-fiction du XVIIe siècle finissant: incapable de reprendre sous forme scientifique le rêve de domination de l'homme sur le monde, la fiction puise à pleines mains dans les légendes populaires et les sciences occultes qui assuraient à l'homme une puissance plus exaltante que celle des machines cartésiennes. [17]

This leads to the next moot point concerning fairy tales — reason versus imagination or how much and what type *merveilleux*. For the study of fairy tales and all imaginative literature, there is prob-

---

[16] Montfaucon de Villars, *Le Comte de Gabalis ou Entretien sur les sciences secrètes* (Paris: A. C. Nize, 1963), *passim,* pp. 78-80.

[17] Villars, p. 44.

ably no other term more important than the French "merveilleux."
It is perhaps best translated by "supernatural" and might even be
equated with "magic" as defined by Tolkien: "The magic of Faerie
is not an end in itself, its virtue is in its operations: among these
are the satisfaction of primordial human desires." [18] With this def-
inition we move into the realm of mythology, for it, too, offers
explanations of such basic human desires as the longing for immortality and for knowledge of natural phenomena. Similarly, in the
seventeenth century myths were found to be synonymous with
fables.

> En 1674, Boileau déclarait que 'la Fable offre à l'esprit
> mille agrémens divers;' par 'la Fable' Boileau entendait,
> comme ses contemporains, la mythologie classique, sans
> l'usage de laquelle, d'après le législateur, 'la poésie est
> morte.' [19]

Hence *merveilleux* might be said to have ramifications in mythology, magic, *féerie,* fables, and the supernatural. In short, it is everything which is contrary to reason. This is the same conclusion
reached by Leibnitz in 1716 when he investigated the *merveilleux*
and found it to be "un refus, délibéré ou inconscient, du ration-
nel . . ." [20] Even in the century of Descartes the public grew bored
with the rationalism of the long realistic novels and turned to the
more imaginative lapidary forms of fables and fairy tales. This is
not a surprising turn in that it was an age in which mythology was
studied by every young noble and the court itself was steeped in
make-believe.

It must be remembered, moreover, that this *merveilleux* did
not originate in the seventeenth century. It was such a real part
of the French way of life that it seemed always to have been
present. It was evident during the Renaissance in the effort to
reconcile Christian and pagan elements and in Platonism, that yearning for something higher intuitively remembered. In the Middle
Ages the *merveilleux* was perhaps at its peak in the *Chansons de
geste* and in the *Lais* of Marie de France. Storer made a distinction
between the *merveilleux* of the two epochs.

---

[18] Tolkien, p. 13.
[19] Delaporte, p. 175.
[20] Soriano, p. 462.

Toutefois, il y a une différence entre la féerie des Romans de la Table Ronde et celle des contes de fées. Celle-là mélange le merveilleux païen et le merveilleux chrétien; l'histoire du Saint Graal est liée aux récits des diableries de Merlin l'Enchanteur. La chronique de Jean d'Arras sur Mélusine confond également les deux sortes de merveilleux. Avec nos contes de fées, il est devenu tout païen, le goût du XVIIe siècle défendant un tel mélange. [21]

Is it not ironic that the fairy tale, whose roots extend back to religious myth, should be the genre which finally banished the Christian *merveilleux*? At the same time it was the genre which developed a new type of *merveilleux* steeped in morality. While Christianity was filled with moral precepts which taught man how to live in God's world, the fairy tale simply replaced God's world with an Other World peopled with good and bad creatures who were rewarded or punished according to their nature. While abandoning the Christian supernatural, the fairy tale, nevertheless, espoused its lessons. One of the most striking examples is the practice of giving one's word. Even the most villainous character always keeps his promises. This reveals the basic optimism toward human nature in folk tales. This optimism is probably one of the reasons for the popularity of the tales through the ages, for human nature, though basically irrational, prefers having its conflicts resolved in a harmonious manner. According to Soriano, it is here that

le merveilleux joue (et ne peut pas ne pas jouer) un rôle de compensation. C'est un des facteurs qui diminuent les tensions, qui assurent tant bien que mal le rapport entre les hommes et la cohérence toujours remise en question de l'ensemble. [22]

It follows that the so-called pagan *merveilleux* took over the role formerly held by Christianity, that of compensator and restorer of hope.

It is here that the French *fée* plays an essential role. The very derivation of the word implies its purpose. The etymology most often mentioned is that it comes from the Latin *fatum* > *fatare* (to enchant). Yet the French *fée* enchants in a very special way. Both

---

[21] Storer, p. 237.
[22] Soriano, p. 475.

Delaporte and Montégut concur that French fairies are different from the Germanic or even the Breton fairy. The following are some of the characteristics attributed to the "bonnes fées françaises" by Montégut:

> Les fées sont humaines, et les âmes sont fées. Voilà le véritable merveilleux français: il est tout moral, contrairement au merveilleux des autres peuples qui prend sa source dans la nature. [23]

He credits them with having intelligence, good sense, and the gift of enchantment. Montégut concludes that "cette transformation des fées en marraines et en protectrices est leur dernière incarnation dans notre pays." [24]

Delaporte believes that "elles sont presque chrétiennes." [25] These miraculous creatures protect their charges, endow them with special qualities, aid those in distress and console others whom they cannot change. Because of them the evil of bad fairies is thwarted at every turn. These French fairies, who were almost always referred to as "bonnes fées" as if it were one word, were so good as to deserve the epithet "angelic." Delaporte, now completely captivated by his subject, finds that "les fées françaises sont agissantes . . . désintéressées, simples, sobres . . ." [26] And if the above mentioned qualities were not quite enough, Delaporte adds that "Ce sont excellement les fées de l'enfance. Ce sont aussi les plus humaines, c'est-à-dire les plus raisonnables." [27] There they are — these special French *fées* who are at the same time human and angelic, Christian and magical, protective and unselfish — truly contradictory, yet utterly charming entities.

To think that the rational seventeenth century would have anything to do with such imaginative forms of literature as those described above is almost incredible. Yet most of us are probably familiar with the idea expressed in Kranz's *Essai sur l'esthétique de Descartes* that the French fairies are Cartesian in that they per-

---

[23] Emile Montégut, "Des Fées et de leur littérature en France," *Revue des Deux Mondes,* 1ᵉʳ avril, 1862, p. 668.
[24] Montégut, p. 670.
[25] Delaporte, p. 76.
[26] Delaporte, p. 79.
[27] Delaporte, p. 82.

form logical enchantments such as selecting a pumpkin, which is round and rolling, to be Cinderella's coach rather than some cylindrical squash or eggplant. Delaporte apparently thinks it matters little whether we find the French fairies Cartesian or not as the *merveilleux* is found "... en dehors des chefs-d'œuvre, chez des écrivains nullement classiques, souvent dans des livres que Boileau eût condamnés à moisir sur les 'rebords du Pont-Neuf.' " [28]

From the vantage point of the twentieth century, J. R. R. Tolkien, noted author of *The Lord of the Rings,* has resolved the old reason versus fantasy dichotomy by making them interdependent. It was in his *Tree and Leaf* that he wrote:

> Fantasy is a natural human activity. It certainly does not destroy or even insult Reason; and it does not either blunt the appetite for, nor obscure the perception of scientific verity. On the contrary. The keener and the clearer is the reason, the better fantasy it will make. [29]

Perhaps this is the real reason for the popularity of the fairy tale in the France of the late seventeenth century. Perhaps they sensed subconsciously what Tolkien put into words nearly three hundred years later, that is that Imagination and Reason ought not be divorced, but rather should be living happily together ever after.

---

[28] Delaporte, p. 60.
[29] Tolkien, p. 54.

CHAPTER II

METHODS OF ANALYZING THE FAIRY TALE

INHERENT IN THE VARIOUS origins of the fairy tales is the approach to be followed in their analysis. Marc Soriano, for example, in his study of Perrault, used almost every approach now known in order to draw from each the clues that would enable him to lay valid proofs leading to his conclusion that Perrault's being a twin made him the real author of the *Histoires du temps passé*. Often some personal bias prevents the critic from finding new meanings or from seeing different elements in a fairy tale or other literary work. If the reader-critic becomes convinced that folktales are derived from Aryan myths, then he will pursue his research in such a manner as to prove his basic tenet. He will look for commonalities between known folktales and myths from which they are supposedly sprung. He may also overlook some rather obvious divergencies between the two in his zeal to establish proof of his own belief. Still, the analyzer must begin somewhere and if the originators of a certain system of investigation had not begun with some sort of hypothesis in order to collect data and classify folktales, we might never have arrived at the point where we are today, for one theory refutes the preceding in order to lay the groundwork for its own doctrine.

The traditional method of interpretation of a work in France has been the biographical study, often referred to as "l'homme et l'œuvre." This approach had its beginning with Sainte-Beuve's much quoted "tel arbre tel fruit" theory in the first half of the nineteenth century. Closely allied to the biographical approach and still under the heading of traditional was Lanson's bibliographical and

chronological method of analysis which we might aptly refer to as
"les sources, c'est tout!" Among the critics of fairy tales who might
be said to follow this manner of interpretation would be Charles
Deulin in *Les Contes de ma mère l'oye avant Perrault,* Jacques
Barchilon in *Perrault's Tales of Mother Goose,* and Sainte-Beuve's
own treatment of Perrault and his tales in his *Lundis* and *Nouveaux
Lundis.* Edmond Pilon, too, used this type of analysis in his *Muses
et bourgeoises de jadis* when he entitled the chapter dealing with
Madame d'Aulnoy "La fée des contes" and portrayed her as a
"grand-maman" telling fairy stories to her grand-children. This
sort of treatment of an author and his work is often shallow, for
it acquaints the reader neither with the work nor with the author.
Marc Soriano, in *Les Contes de Perrault,* stated that the usual analysis, that is *l'homme et l'œuvre,* was not suitable for discussing the
fairy tale because of the divergent opinions about its genre, its
audience and its origin. However, if this approach could be coupled
with one of the more recent textual studies, it would doubtless
offer the best means of analyzing fairy tales or other works.

The Mythological and Philological schools of thought approach
the study of folktales in approximately the same way; so they will
be dealt with as one. Their primary goal is to discover the original
source of folktales. Their approach consists of collecting and com-
paring tales from different countries to determine their common
origin. One group, the Orientalists, even presented ample proof
that the original home of European folktales was India. According
to Joseph Bédier,

> Ceux-ci croient en possession d'une idée directrice, qu'ils
> considèrent comme déjà démontrée. Ils poursuivent leurs
> collections à l'abri de cette croyance: les contes viennent
> de l'Inde. Pour ceux qu'on retrouve en Orient, c'est la
> forme orientale qui est primitive; pour les autres, on trou-
> vera quelque jour cette forme; elle a existé, ou existe;
> et l'on a prouvé, disent-ils, l'origine indienne de tant de
> contes que nous pouvons dès maintenant admettre la même
> origine pour les autres. Cette foi est un mol oreiller d'in-
> curiosité, qui permet de se livrer plus longtemps aux joies
> du collectionneur. [1]

---

[1] Joseph Bédier, *Les Fabliaux* (Paris: Librairie Ancienne Edouard Champion, 1925), p. 253.

As mentioned in Chapter I, it was Bédier who discredited the Indian theory by proving the tales had a plurality of origins:

> La polygenèse des contes nous est attestée par mille exemples: des centaines de légendes religieuses, sentimentales, merveilleuses, sont propres à tel pays, non à tels autres. [2]

The other groups of Mythologists endeavor to establish that popular tales are only transformations of primitive myths. The principal difference between the Aryans, Max Müller and the Grimms and the Anthropologist Andrew Lang is that the former, as their name implies, are of the opinion that these myths were those of their own Indo-European ancestors. The Anthropologists, on the other hand, judge that the tales derive from ancient myths of a primitive epoch — "la sauvagerie." Again, it is Bédier who best describes their efforts:

> La méthode pour les étudier consiste à en chercher le noyau mythique, en applicant les règles de la philologie comparée, à le dépouiller de sa gangue d'éléments adventices et à déterminer les transformations graduelles du mythe primitif. [3]

The choice of matter studied by the Anthropologist differs from the Mythologist, both solar and primitive, in that his scope is wider and his analysis is in more depth. He is interested in taboos, fetishes, totemisms, superstitions, mores, transformations — anything and everything that has to do with primitive man's social, religious or private ways of life. His objective is to understand thoroughly the savage mind that created the basic human beliefs and fears behind the universal myths. Writers such as Andrew Lang (*Myth, Ritual* and *Religion*), and Macleod Yearsley (*The Folklore of the Fairy Tale*) exemplify the type of detailed study the Anthropologist carries out.

One of Bédier's strongest points was that we can never known for sure when we have found the original source and even if we do think we have found it in the *Pantchatantra* or the *Roman de Sept Sages,* we can never ascertain whether the writers of these

---

[2] Bédier, p. 273.
[3] Bédier, p. 57.

works borrowed motifs from oral tradition and, in turn, influenced later writers. His arguments are so logical and cogent that we find ourselves in wholehearted agreement with his view that we shall never learn how or when these tales arose nor how they were propagated. Moreover, it is of little import whether we learn it or not.

Bédier is classified as an Ethnologist because of his belief that one can only trace the origins of purely ethnic folktales. The Ethnologist does not approach the study of folktales by the comparison method of the Philologists and Mythologists; rather he concentrates on earlier forms in order to show how they exhibit special traits or sentiments common only to one people. He makes a compilation of popular tales from one culture and, one by one, inspects the organic traits that tie them to a particular culture as they evolved. Such is the goal of Bédier in *Les Fabliaux.*

The folklorists are collectors and organizers of tales. They have provided the scholar with one of the most useful tools available for the study of folktales — the Aarne-Thompson *Motif-Index of Folk-Literature,* designed basically for the folk narratives of Europe. The tales are listed under the following rubrics:

> A. Mythological Motifs
> B. Animals
> C. Tabu
> D. Magic (Fairy tales are a subclass — tales of magic)
> E. The Dead
> F. Marvels
> G. Ogres
> H. Tests
> J. The Wise and the Foolish
> K. Deceptions
> L. Reversal of Fortune
> M. Ordaining the Future
> N. Chance and Fate
> P. Society
> Q. Rewards and Punishment
> R. Captives and Fugitives
> S. Unnatural Cruelty
> T. Sex
> U. Nature of Life
> V. Religion

X. Traits of Character
Y. Humor
Z. Miscellaneous Motifs [4]

From these headings we can judge the contribution such an under-
taking has made. While the alphabetical index in Volume VI may
be used for tracing motifs, Thompson indicates in the introduction
that he hopes its main use will be for cataloguing. His is a simple
structure which arranges all the motifs together that treat the same
subject. Richard Dorson commented in his introduction to Geneviève Massignon's *Folktales of France* that

> Since the Aarne-Thompson index can give but a bare figure
> for the number of versions of a given tale type reported
> in each country, national indexes are needed as supple-
> ments in an ingenious interlocking apparatus. For the
> French catalogue, Delarue planned a sensible and informa-
> tive scheme. Each tale type is given first its Aarne-Thomp-
> son number and title, then the text of a representative
> French variant, then a breakdown of the main divisions
> and episodes of the *conte,* and finally a tabulated list of
> versions with bibliographical sources and notes on devi-
> ations from the main form and a summary statement on
> studies of the tale and its world-wide distribution. [5]

To the folklorist oral tradition looms important. Many collections of stories from specific regions and professions, such as the
basket makers' tales from Haute Bretagne (Ariane de Félice), have
appeared. The new techniques of tale collecting employed by folklorists such as Paul Sébillot, Arnold van Gennep, Henry Gaidoz,
and Geneviève Massignon involve the teller, the style, the dialect
as well as the text. Many have traveled to remote regions with
their tape recorders in order to set down the oral tradition in its
original setting and dialect. Their work is then collected and put in
print in series such as *Folktales of the World* edited by Richard
M. Dorson.

After any study of oral tradition it is imperative to look at
"les livres de colportage" or chapbooks for "Quelque littérature

---

[4] Stith Thompson, *Motif-Index of Folk-Literature,* Vol. I (Bloomington:
Indiana University, 1955), pp. 29-35.

[5] Massignon, p. xxx.

que l'on écrive, on trouve d'abord des chanteurs et des conteurs, plus tard des écrivains."[6] Even though this type of literature has not always been esteemed in literary circles, its influence is nonetheless great. It offered to a certain reading public simple stories similar to the ones they had possibly heard as a child. At the same time

> La littérature diffusée par les colporteurs représente un aspect non négligeable de la tradition nationale de la France. Elle en marque une étape et, bien qu'actuellement elle soit totalement disparue, elle constitue un élément de la formation de la sensibilité esthétique du peuple français et par là de sa culture nationale.[7]

These little books were more popular in the north where they apparently aided in unifying the language. This might be considered a detriment to the folklorists who are seeking to find areas where the dialect, as well as the folklore, has remained intact.

It seems as if one development followed close on another and was predicated on the findings of the preceding method. Hence the folklorists followed the lead of the Ethnologists within national and even regional studies and collections. The stylistic and textual comparisons resulted from the folklorists' probings. For example, Vladimir Propp, in his *Morphology of the Folktale,* began by criticizing the Aarne index: "The works of this school proceed from the unconscious premise that each plot is something organically whole, that it can be singled out from a number of other plots and studied independently."[8] Propp's method of investigation suggests that the proper study of folktales is through small component parts. He begins with four basic theses and sets out to prove them deductively. They are as follows:

> 1. Functions serve as stable, constant elements in folktales, independent of who performs them and how they are fulfilled by the dramatis personae. They constitute the components of a folktale.

---

[6] Brochon, p. 9.

[7] Brochon, p. 9.

[8] Vladimir Propp, *Morphology of the Folktale,* ed. by S. Pirkova-Jakobson, trans. Laurence Scott (Bloomington: Indiana University, 1958), p. 8.

2. The number of functions known in the fairy tale is limited.

3. The sequence of functions is always identical.

4. All fairy tales, by their structure, belong to one and the same type.[9]

It is important to understand what Propp meant by function. For his interpretation it is taken to be an act of dramatis personae. Later in the present work we shall subject some of Mme. d'Aulnoy's *contes* to a similar analysis to determine what similarities exist among the characters and what themes emerge. Surely an approach which begins with decomposition into components will lend itself easily to works of Descartes' era.

Perhaps the most fascinating analyses have come from the Psychoanalytical school, for their interpretations of dreams and fairy tales are steeped in symbolism; and ours is an age which enjoys the process of deciphering symbols and analyzing the subconscious. Even though we broach it with scepticism, we soon realize that it, too, is not without some merit in elucidating the meaning of fairy tales. Yet, those who espouse this technique often become so eager to interpret symbols and discover archetypes that they carry their analyses too far and thereby they lose credence. Whereas Propp was primarily interested in functions of the characters, Jung is mainly concerned with archetypes which he defines as manifestations of instinctive physiological urges revealed through symbolic images. In *The Archetypes and the Collective Unconscious* Jung states the function of archetypes:

> For that (unification of the personality) not only in fairy tales but in life generally, the objective intervention of the archetype is needed, which checks the purely affective reactions with a chain of inner confrontations and realizations. These cause the who? where? how? why? to emerge clearly and in this wise bring knowledge of the immediate situation as well as of the goal. The resultant enlightenment and untying of the fatal tangle often has something positively magical about it — an experience not unknown to the psychotherapist.[10]

---

[9] Propp, pp. 20-21.
[10] *The Collected Works of C. G. Jung,* trans. R. F. C. Hull, Vol. IX, Part I (London: Routledge and Kegan Paul, 1959), p. 220.

Through fairy tales and dreams Man is led to what is innate in the psyche. The discovery of this other self or other world is instrumental in the process of individuation or maturation, for this realization brings totality or wholeness to the individual. Loeffler-Delachaux adds another purpose of the archetypes:

> L'absence des archétypes ou "images ancestrales" dénonce d'une manière absolument claire le conte truqué ou le conte inventé par des auteurs naïfs qui ont cru pouvoir substituer leur propre imagination aux produits du psychisme universel. [11]

It will be interesting to test this statement on some of Mme. d'Aulnoy's tales to see whether she substituted her own imagination in lieu of the deeper ancestral images.

Loeffler-Delachaux finds three levels of interpretation of language and symbols which she expresses clearly in the following schema:

Au degré	nous nous exprimons	Au moyen	à l'état	Ces états correspondent:
Profane	le langage	des mots	de veille	à notre inconscient
Sacré	le rêve	Images symboliques	de sommeil	à notre inconscient individuel
Initiatique	les mythes les légendes contes de fées	mots magiques, incantations	inspiration, transe médiumnique	à notre inconscient collectif [12]

By extension, she defines fairies on the intiatic level. "Les fées sont les 'fates' ou les 'vates,' initiés druidiques des deux sexes, du troisième dégre." [13] Loeffler-Delachaux concludes that the fairy tale addresses itself to our unconscious and it is understood only through

---

[11] Marguerite Loeffler-Delachaux, *Le Symbolisme des contes de fées* (Paris: l'Arche, 1949), p. 47.

[12] Loeffler-Delachaux, p. 52.

[13] Loeffler-Delachaux, p. 235.

intuition. We might add that women are reputed to be more highly endowed with this quality and might therefore be in a better position not only to interpret the tales, but to set them down as well.

The Psychoanalytical analysis delves deeply into the subconscious in order to arrive at a satisfactory explanation of symbols in fairy tales. Naturally, they deal with primordial desires which are too private to be expressed overtly so they are revealed covertly through symbols in myths, legends and fairy tales. Since these basic desires expressed in symbols are common to all men in all ages, Jung says they belong to a collective unconscious. The deciphering process for the psychological interpretation lies somewhere between a totally subjective or objective truth of the symbol. It is well known that since Freud these truths have been founded on the level of sexual activity and arrived at through free association.

> The critic substitutes for that method an association of passages from the author in question, patiently collected and grouped together as evidence of related themes, images, metaphors that reveal important constructions of the subconscious. [14]

Jung, however, narrowed the field of free association so as not to be led too far astray from the original allegorical image. It might be well to stop here to clarify some of Jung's terminology:

> An *allegory* is a paraphrase of a conscious content, whereas a *symbol* is the best possible expression for an unconscious content whose nature can only be guessed, because it is still unknown. [15]

The Jungian *archetype* is also on the unconscious level but differs from the symbol in that it explains the world by reference to man while the symbol is more on the cosmic plane. The distinction Jung makes here is parallel to the familiar microcosm = macrocosm or what is above is like what is below.

In summary, the statement of Munro S. Edmonson concerning the Psychological method of interpretation offers the most logical point of view at this time:

---

[14] Wallace Fowlie, *The French Critic 1549-1967* (Carbondale and Edwardsville: Southern Illinois University Press, 1968), p. 92.

[15] Jung, p. 6 (footnote).

A Freudian "reading" of myths and tales is not a substitute for other modes of interpretation and analysis, but it is an invaluable supplement. It is not more "real" but it is as "real" and cannot be overlooked. [16]

The final method of analysis to be treated here is the Thematic. It differs from the Psychoanalytic in that it bases its findings on textual proofs rather than intuition. According to Fowlie:

> *Thematic* is a newer word than *theme,* and it is used precisely by the new critic, by a Richard for example, to indicate that there are themes in a literary work of whose meaning he is not absolutely sure, about which he has no absolute knowledge. [17]

Thematic analysis differs from the study of themes as it was carried out in the nineteenth century in that it allows for many themes and does not pursue one theme as if it were the author's sole intent. In this paper *thematic* will refer, as it does in the new criticism, to an emphasis on the work rather than on the author. Therefore, Mme. d'Aulnoy as an individual will interest us only in so far as she is involved in her works. In our investigation of her *contes de fées* we shall explore several of the methods discussed above, but the primary emphasis will ever be on arriving at a comprehensive and conclusive analysis of the tales themselves.

---

[16] Monro S. Edmonson, *Lore, An Introduction to the Science of Folklore and Literature* (New York: Holt, Rinehart and Winston, 1971), p. 219.
[17] Fowlie, p. 124.

CHAPTER III

"ZEITGEIST" IN MME. D'AULNOY'S *CONTES DES FÉES*

MADAME D'AULNOY [1] wrote twenty-five fairy tales. Her first, "Le Prince Adolphe et la princesse Félicité," was interpolated in her first novel, *L'Histoire d'Hypolite, Comte de Duglas* in the year 1690. Because of this first tale which preceded Perrault's *Histoires ou Contes du temps passé,* she has often been referred to as the innovator of literary fairy tales. Her other twenty-four tales were published in eight volumes as *Les Contes des fées* in 1697 and *Les Contes Nouveaux ou les Fées à la Mode* in 1698. Storer maintains that "six des huit volumes des premières éditions des contes de Mme d'Aulnoy sont introuvables." [2]

Mme. d'Aulnoy believed that she would be remembered for her more realistic works — her *Mémoires,* her novels or her *Relation du Voyage d'Espagne* rather than for her lighter works of fantasy. Yet, one who begins a study of Mme. d'Aulnoy's fairy tales soon learns that she is known best for these fairy tales, some of which are still read by children today, [3] and for her *Relation du Voyage d'Espagne.* However well she may be known and appreciated for her *contes de fées,* there is relatively little written specifically about the tales. Most writers treat her in a general fashion along with other women writers of fairy tales in the late seventeenth century. Storer, for example, whose goal was to explain the interest in the genre in the

---

[1] See Appendix I for a chronological résumé of Mme. d'Aulnoy's life.
[2] Storer, p. 254.
[3] The recent catalog, *French Books, A Comprehensive Guide to the Selection of French Books* (New York: French Book Corporation of America, 1973), lists three works by Mme. d'Aulnoy — *Contes* and *Relation du Voyage d'Espagne* (p. 68) and an Age d'or Album, *La Princesse Fanette* [sic] (p. 12).

waning years of Louis XIV's reign rather than perform a detailed analysis of Mme. d'Aulnoy's tales, summarized the works and the author by saying:

> Les critiques les plus avisés d'aujourd'hui donnent à Mme d'Aulnoy sa juste place, la considérant comme le plus célèbre de tous les auteurs de contes après Perrault, avec les qualités et les défauts de son sexe — une abondante et riche imagination, un style aisé et naturel, quelquefois négligé, un luxe de détails pittoresques qui traînent trop en longueur, un esprit salonnier, des figures "de tendre porcelaine" qu'on ne doit pas trop remuer de peur de les casser, une élégance qui annonce le xviiie siècle, et avec cela, une fine ironie, une philosophie quelque peu sombre, une veine de cruauté qui vous inquiète légèrement, lorsque vous pensez à la vie de l'auteur, mais qui est compensée par une morale assez bien soutenue. Joint à tout cela, elle a une connaissance sympathique des animaux, vraiment remarquable dans une femme de salon, inspirée en cela par Mme Deshoulières, sinon par La Fontaine. Mme d'Aulnoy est celle qui, à l'avant-garde, annonce le siècle de Watteau, introduisante le merveilleux dans les salons de la fin du grand regne, gardant en même temps le rationalisme classique et le souci de la morale, étant toujours précieuse, généralement de la bonne préciosité, appartenant au grand siècle par un mélange continuel de bel esprit et de cartésianisme. [4]

There are no textual examples from Mme. d'Aulnoy's tales which point up her "style aisé et naturel," her "abondante et riche imagination," her "esprit salonnier" or even her "fine ironie." Since the advent of new criticism (long after Miss Storer's treatise), readers have come to expect textual proof and to delight in exploring repetitious motifs leading to themes in a work.

Dunlop, too, deals with a few of her tales in a very general way. His principal concern is with their origin.

> Mme. d'Aulnoy's fairy tale of *Belle-Etoile* has been copied either from the Arabian or Italian. Indeed all the best fairy tales of that lady, as well as most others which com-

---

[4] Storer, p. 41.

pose the *Cabinet des Fées,* are mere translations of the *Nights of Straparola.*[5]

It is interesting to study the origins of the tales and make comparisons among the different versions, but for an in-depth analysis of the tales themselves, this offers little of immediate value. The fullest treatment of the *Contes des fées* is found in a German dissertation by Kurt Krüger in 1914. He organizes the tales in two large groups, breaking them down and fitting them all into one of the chosen areas. In his first group called *Volksmärchen* (folk tales), he lists "La Belle aux cheveux d'or," "La Princesse Rosette," "La Bonne Petite Souris," "Finette Cendron," "L'Oranger et l'abeille" and "La Chatte blanche." In the second group labeled *Kunstmärchen* (art tales), he places all the others fitting them under the genre to which they are best suited. There are five *Sentimental Marchen*: "Le Prince Adolphe et la Princesse Gluck," "Le Mouton," "La Princesse Belle Etoile et le Prince Chéri," "La Biche au Bois," "L'Oiseau bleu"; three *Galante Märchen*: "Belle-Belle ou le Chevalier Fortuné," "Le Prince Lutin," "Gracieuse et Percinet"; three *Scherzhafte Märchen* (joking): "Le Dauphin," "Le Prince Marcassin" and "La Princesse Printanière"; three *Schäferliche Märchen* (bucolic): "La Princesse Carpillon," "Le Rameau d'or," and "Le Pigeon et la Colombe"; and finally five *Wunderbare Märchen* (wonder): "Le Serpentin vert," "Fortunée," "Le Nain jaune," "La Grenouille bienfaisante" and "Babiole."[6] Krüger admits that these are arbitrary groupings on his part and that Mme. d'Aulnoy drew no such sharp divisions in her stories. His groupings helped him to prove his major premise that there were two diverse elements struggling in Mme. d'Aulnoy — tradition versus aesthetic refinement. He concludes that the more she refines, the less she appeals to the reader.[7]

The aim of the present study is to examine all twenty-five of Madame d'Aulnoy's *contes de fées* in order to derive which were her major themes and what were the characteristics of her writing

---

[5] John Dunlop, *The History of Fiction* (London: Reeves and Turner, 1876), p. 270.

[6] Kurt Krüger, *Die Märchen der Baronin Aulnoy,* Inaugural-Dissertation (Leipzig, 1914), pp. 66-116.

[7] Krüger, *passim,* pp. 86-89.

that gave her reputation of being "le plus célèbre de tous les auteurs de contes après Perrault."

Mme. d'Aulnoy was a child of her time. According to Jeanne Roche-Mazon,

> Elle tenait salon. Elle mariait fort bien ses filles, dédiait des livres à de grandes princesses et allait hardiment se plaindre au lieutenant de police lorsqu'on lui imputait des écrits scandaleux. [8]

She was quite familiar with court life and all of its political intrigues. It seems apparent, too, that she was equally versed in the amatory affairs of the period, if we are to believe most reports. Jal has often been quoted as saying that she was a lady whose "désordres de sa conduite ont rendue aussi célèbre que ses ouvrages." [9]

Just what are the facets of seventeenth-century French life depicted in Mme. d'Aulnoy's fairy tales? First of all, her tales have noble personages without exception. Her heroes or heroines might be transformed temporarily into some lower social stratum, or even into an animal, but, in the end, all are noble. In fact, all of her tales except one begin "Il y avait (or "Il était") une fois un roi et une reine." Even "Fortunée," the one tale that begins "Il était une fois un pauvre laboureur," has a heroine who turns out to be a princess instead of a poor laborer's daughter. The heroes maintain their virtuous demeanor even under metamorphosis. Two prime examples are "Babiole" and "Le Prince Marcassin." [10] Both are bewitched by evil fairies at birth. Babiole is the princess born a monkey whose parents send her to be drowned. She is rescued by her aunt as a pet for her son. At her aunt's court Babiole amazes everyone by her appearance and her intelligence.

> La reine lui donne des maîtres que exercèrent bien la vivacité de son esprit; elle excellait à jouer du clavecin: on lui en avait fait un merveilleux dans une huître à l'écaille: il venait des peintres des quatre parties du monde, et particulièrement d'Italie, pour la peindre; sa renommée volait

---

[8] Jeanne Roche-Mazon, *Autour des contes de fées* (Paris: Didier, 1968), p. 150.

[9] Auguste Jal, *Dictionnaire critique de biographie et d'histoire,* 2d ed. (Paris: Henri Plon, 1872), p. 1306.

[10] For full resumes of the twenty-five tales, see Appendix II.

d'un pôle à l'autre, car on n'avait point encore vu une guenon qui parlât. . . . Babiole avait un cœur, et ce cœur n'avait pas été métamorphosé comme le reste de sa petite personne: elle prit donc de la tendresse pour le prince, et il en prit si fort qu'il en prit trop.[11]

Babiole's talents and accomplishments are those that the seventeenth century tried to inculcate in its young ladies, wit in conversation, musical ability and morality. The fact that her heart has not been transformed enables her to experience human love for her cousin. Love, that sentiment which occupied so fully the seventeenth-century courtesans, was discussed, written about and even experienced in all of its myriad forms. That a monkey princess learns to love a human prince does not shock us, for Babiole never really becomes an animal in the reader's eye. She has all the courtly virtues and human characteristics. "Quelle merveille! Babiole parlante, Babiole raisonnante! " (I, p. 267). The minute she begins to talk she also begins to reason. That, too, is typical of the century that produced Descartes. As soon as she learns to talk and to reason, she recounts later that "l'on me donna des maîtres qui m'apprirent plusieurs langues" (I, p. 278). The interest in languages coupled with the vogue for foreign travel added another dimension of seventeenth-century life to Mme. d'Aulnoy's works. There had been a steady stream of Italian artisans in France since the Renaissance. Did not these Italian painters come to paint the charming Babiole? Because of the intermarriage of European royalty, there was a constant flow of travel between the various courts and it was only natural that this would develop an interest in other languages. It seems uncertain whether Mme. d'Aulnoy herself spoke any other languages, but there is no denying that she was interested in languages as evidenced by her constant references to words and her use of unusual expressions in her *Contes* and in her *Relation du Voyage d'Espagne*. This element of her works will be discussed later.

Marcassin, the princely boar, like Babiole, is to the manner born.

---

11 Madame d'Aulnoy, *Les Contes des fées*, Vol. I (Paris: Mercure de France, 1956), p. 268. All textual quotations are from this edition of the *Contes*.

Il était né avec un esprit supérieur, et un courage intré-
pide. Le roi connaissant son caractère, commença à l'aimer
plus qu'il n'avait fait jusque-là. Il choisit de bons maîtres
pour lui apprendre tout ce qu'on pourrait. Il réussissait
mal aux danses figurées, mais pour le passe-pied et le me-
nuet où il fallait aller vite et légèrement, il y faisait des
merveilles. A l'égard des instruments, il connut bien que
le luth et le théorbe ne lui convenaient pas; il aimait la
guitare, et jouait joliment de la flûte. Il montait à cheval
avec une disposition et une grâce surprenantes; il ne se
passait guère de jours qu'il n'allât à la chasse, et qu'il ne
donnât de terribles coups de dents aux bêtes les plus féroces
et les plus dangéreuses. Ses maîtres lui trouvaient un esprit vive, et toute la facilité possible à se perfectionner
dans les sciences. (II, p. 289)

From this passage one would never know this was a fairy tale nor
that the young creature being discussed was a boar. This might be
a description of one of the heroes in the works of Mme. de La
Fayette, Mme. de Villedieu or any of the other historico-sentimental
novelists of the period. It is easy to see that the young gentleman
has to learn not only the refinement which would permit him to
acquit himself in any courtly situation with the women, but the
manly arts of riding and hunting as well. He, too, learns to speak
"...comme font tous les enfants, il bégayait un peu" (II, p. 289).
When he asks permission of his mother to marry a young lady who
is at court, his mother replies that he can wed her only if the young
lady will consent freely to wed him without feeling any pressure
from his high position. Marcassin retorts:

Je vous assure, madame lui dit Marcassin, avec un air fan-
faron, que vous êtes la seule qui pensiez si desavantageuse-
ment de moi; je ne vois personne qui ne me loue, et ne
me fasse apercevoir que j'ai mille bonnes qualités.
—Tels sont des courtisans, dit la reine, et telle est la
condition des princes, les uns louent toujours, les autres
sont toujours loués; comment connaître ses défauts dans
un tel labyrinthe? (II, p. 301)

If we read this without knowing when it was written or by whom,
we would easily deduce that it was from the period of Louis XIV
and we might guess that it was written by a La Rochefoucauld or
a Molière, for it clearly depicts the attitude of the moralists toward

court flattery. Mme. d'Aulnoy's characters are imbued with the attitudes of seventeenth-century France concerning morality. This is why so many of her critics refer to her "esprit salonnier" and her "préciosité."

There are other references to court life in "Le Prince Marcassin" when he decides to leave the court for a milieu better suited to his boarish instincts. In the forest he meets the third sister who says she will marry him if he will return to court. He quickly refuses, adding:

> Ne croyez pas, jeune Marthésie, que ce soit toujours une brillante cour qui fasse notre félicité la plus solide, il est des douceurs plus charmantes, et je vous le répète. (II, p. 308)

One would think from such statements that Mme. d'Aulnoy was embittered toward the petty happenings at court. Perhaps it was because of her own involvement in so many intrigues that she could speak so positively about pleasures away from court. Besides her own conspiracy with her mother against her husband, Foulché-Delbosc mentioned that Mme. d'Aulnoy was "compromise par une liaison suspecte avec Mme. Carlier-Ticquet, et menacée de la suivre sur l'échafaud." [12]

The tales also relate some of the court amusements enjoyed by the nobles at their celebrations. At Prince Lutin's wedding,

> cinq ou six volumes ne suffiraient point pour décrire les opéras, les courses de bagues, les musiques, les combats de gladiateurs, les chasses et les autres magnificences qu'il y eut à ces charmantes noces. (I, p. 111)

Babiole, too, enjoys the "courses de bagues" along with other pastimes.

> ... Elle se divertissait à voir courre la bague, dont elle donnait toujours le prix, au jeu, à la comédie, à la chasse, car l'on avait conduit une rivière. (I, p. 281)

---

[12] Quoted in Foulché-Delbosc, "Madame d'Aulnoy et l'Espagne," in Mme. d'Aulnoy, *Relation du Voyage d'Espagne* (Paris: Klincksieck, 1926), p. 22.

Other *contes* mention types of dances that were performed at court. The opening paragraph of "La Bonne petite souris" lists many court divertissements, among them were "danser la bourrée et la pavane"[13] (I, p. 207). The "chatte blanche" entertains her prince by having "douze chats et singes qui dansèrent un ballet. Les uns étaient vêtus en Maures, et les autres en Chinois" (II, p. 116). This latter reference to dressing in oriental fashion was popular in this period. It recalls Molière's Turkish scene in *Le Bourgeois Gentilhomme*. It is only a few years later that Voltaire and Montesquieu will be using visitors from other planets or countries to point out the foibles of French society and its curious attitude toward foreigners. Perhaps the most appealing description of the dances of the time was the one involving the dancing water in "La Princesse Belle-Etoile et le Prince Chéri."

Il fut étrangement surpris de voir que cette eau dansait avec la même justesse que si Favier et Pecout[14] lui avaient montré. Il est vrai que ce n'était que de vieilles danses, comme la Bocane, la Mariée, et la Sarabande.[15] (II, p. 262)

---

[13] "Bourrée: A court dance of the 16th century related to the polka. It originated among the peasants of the Aubergne and consisted of a skipping step." *The Dance Encyclopedia*, Compiled and ed. by Anatole Chujoy and P. W. Manchester (New York: Simon and Schuster, 1967), p. 152.

"Pavane: (Pavin, Panicin) 17th-century dance, name derived either from town of Padua or from Pavo meaning peacock. It is probably the latter as ladies swept their trains in the dance in the manner of a peacock parading his tail. There were many curtsies, retreats and advances in the Pavanne, and the lady rested her hand on the back of man's. Poses were held and the style was dignified and aloof. The dance was set in 2/4 time. It was most popular in Italy, France, and Spain" (p. 712).

[14] "Pécourt, Louis (also spelled Pécour) (1665-1729), French dancer who danced leading roles in Jean Baptiste Lully's and Pierre Beauchamp's ballets. After Beauchamp left the Opera, Pécourt arranged the choreography for a number of ballets and composed dances for Louis XIV. He has been credited with being the actual author of Feuillet's *Choreographie*. He made his first appearance at the Opera in 1672 in the ballet *Cadmus* and was demicaractere in style. He was noted for precision, grace, and lightness. Personally he was a very acceptable man and mixed in the best society of the time." *The Dance Encyclopedia*, p. 717.

[15] "*Bocane* (ca. 1640), a sedate dance in 2/4 time for two people. It was named for the teacher Bocan, who was dancing master to Anne of Austria and to Charles I of England." *The Dance Encyclopedia*, p. 141.

"Sarabande (in Span., La Zarabanda), a dance of Moorish origin which came from Spain in the 12th century. The name comes from an Arabic word meaning noise. Originally it was danced in groups to the accompaniment of

All of these dances were popular during the seventeenth century. The fact that Mme. d'Aulnoy mentions them frequently in the tales would indicate that she took part in many of the court entertainments and evidently enjoyed the dances more than the games, for she makes fewer references to games. One that she does mention is in "Le Dauphin" when the queen welcomes Alcidor to their court. "Elle s'informa même s'il jouait quelquefois, et lui dit de venir tailler à la bassette"[16] (II, p. 322). When not gambling or observing the ballets or other works of fantasy, the court also took pleasure in enacting their own make-believe. The beautiful daughter in "Le Nain jaune" is a good example — "on la voyait toujours vêtue en Pallas ou en Diane, suivie des premières dames de la cour habillées en nymphes" (I, p. 291). One can imagine the young shepherdess parading through the gardens of Versailles followed closely by her admiring nymphs. Emile Magne depicted this same scene in *Les Plaisirs et les Fêtes en France au XVIIe siècle* when he wrote of the *salonniers* of the Hotel de Rambouillet strolling through the gardens to the accompaniment of violin music. They would come upon a rock or a fountain with several members dressed as "Diane chasseresse et en nymphs des bois."[17]

The best listing of seventeenth-century interests, however, appears in "Serpentin vert" when the ugly princess has been taken to the island of the *pagodes,* those charming little creatures who are not allowed to laugh at all the foolish things they see when they go out in the world so that they puff up instead. In order to keep her from growing bored, they visit all the courts and bring back the news.

Il n'y avait point d'heure où quelques pagodes n'arrivassent et ne lui rendissent compte des choses les plus secrètes et les plus curieuses qui se passaient dans le monde:

---

bells and castanets. It was wild in manner and only women participated. In France the sarabande became more subdued and was danced as a solo by either a man or a woman. It was in 3/4 time and chief step consisted of a quick shift from the toe-out to toe-in, characteristic movement of oriental dancing; the rest was slow glides." *The Dance Encyclopedia,* p. 801.

[16] "...la bassette, inventée par l'italien Bassetti et introduite à la cour par Justiniani, l'ambassadeur de Florence." Georges Mongrédien, *La Vie quotidienne sous Louis XIV* (Paris: Hachette, 1948), p. 103.

[17] Emile Magne, *Les Plaisirs et les Fêtes en France au XVIIe siècle* (Genève: Editions de la Frégate, 1944), p. 178.

des traités de paix, des ligues pour faire la guerre, trahisons et ruptures d'amants, infidelités de maîtresses, désespoirs, racommodement, héritiers déçus, mariages rompus, vieilles veuves qui se remariaient fort mal à propos, trésors découverts, banqueroutes, fortunes faites en un moment; favoris tombés, sièges de places, maris jaloux, femmes coquettes, mauvais enfants, villes abimées; enfin que ne venaient-ils pas dire à la princesse pour la réjouir ou pour l'occuper? (I, p. 320)

This was an age interested in the art of conversation, and everything that took place at court became the focal point of many of these conversations. The account given by the *pagodes* gives us a good idea of what they may have discussed in the salons when they were not reading literary works or telling fairy tales.

Mme. d'Aulnoy often refers to names of real people and places in her tales. We have seen that the dancer Pecout, whom she mentioned in "Belle-Etoile et le Prince Chéri," was well-known in the best society of the time. In "Le Prince Lutin" the invisible spirit goes to Paris to try to find some monkeys, for the princess he loves has expressed a desire to have some. "...Il alla ensuite chez Brioché,[18] le fameux joueur de marionnettes, il y trouva deux singes de mérite" (I, p. 100): Mme. d'Aulnoy could have seen and known Pecout and Brioché at court. If she didn't know them, she had heard enough about them to know they were masters in their respective fields. She also mentioned an even more famous person in "Belle-Belle ou le chevalier Fortuné." The queen had composed some verses which "elle fit mettre en musique par le Lully de sa cour" (II, p. 166). As if every court had a Lully!

---

[18] "Brioché (Les Datelin, dits) bateleurs parisiens. Pierre (né en 1567, mort à Paris le 25 sept. 1671 à 105 ans) était joueur d'instruments vers 1618, montreur de marionnettes au Château-Gaillard, près de la Porte de Nesles en 1649 ... François, dit Franchon. Celui-ci naquit le 9 sept. 1620. C'était lui, sans doute, qui montrait les marionnettes à la Foire S.-Germain en 1657 et qui, au cours d'une tournée en Suisse, se fit arrêter à Soleure comme magicien. En 1669 il s'intitulait joueur des ménus plaisirs de Mgr le Dauphin; en 1671 operateur de la Maison du roi, ce qui prouve qu'il était aussi dentiste. Il obtint de jouer à la Foire S.-Germain le 16 oct. 1676 et mourut le 31 mars 1681. Boileau mentionne sa boutique. C'est probablement lui qui était proprietaire du singe Fagotin, que Cyrano de Bergerac tua, dit-on, le prenant pour un homme." *Dictionnaire de biographie française,* Vol. 7, sous la direction de J. Balteau, M. Barroux, et M. Prevoste (Paris: Librairie Le Touzey et Ané, 1933), p. 331.

Some of the places mentioned in the tales reflect their specialties too. For example, the painters from Italy in "Babiole" were much appreciated in the seventeenth century. In "Finette Cendron," when the prince is ill, they look for a doctor "même jusqu'à Paris et à Montpellier" (I, p. 250). The Faculty of Medicine at Montpellier was a place of renown even in Alexander Neckam's day, for he mentioned a friend who was expecting to take up medicine there. [19] In "Belle-Belle ou le chevalier Fortunée" Grugeon, the great bread-eater, consumes so much bread "qu'encore qu'il eût plus de soixante mille pains de Gonesse [20] devant lui, il parassait résolu de n'en pas laisser un seul petit morceau" (II, p. 159). One would hardly call Grugeon "délicat," but he evidently appreciates the fine quality of this special bread from Gonesse.

The inclusion of so many names of people and places adds not only the spirit of the time — Zeitgeist — but a certain realism to the *contes*. Mme. d'Aulnoy's tales are realistic; even amid all the *merveilleux* she incorporates side by side such real details. Much of her realism deals simply with human nature. It might be a young prince who is born a boar and is never expected to talk. Yet, when he does begin to speak, "comme font tous les enfants, il bégayait un peu" (II, p. 289). A stuttering boar is certainly out of the ordinary, but the matter-of-fact manner of presenting his impediment makes him human and real. In fact, the whole story of "Le Prince Marcassin" is a mélange of the real and the unreal. It is the inter-mingling of these two elements that makes Mme. d'Aulnoy's *contes* special. It could be because she adheres to the principle of writing fairy tales that Max Lüthi described. "Everything complex in real-ity is simplified in the fairy tale." [21] Certainly her realism is true to life as seen in "La Princesse Carpillon." The ex-king and queen have been leading a pastoral life and taking care of two foster children — a boy and a girl. They do not object to the love existing be-tween the two young people until they learn that Carpillon, the girl, is their own lost daughter.

---

[19] Urban Tigner Homes, *Daily Living in the Twelfth Century* (Madison: University of Wisconsin Press, 1964), p. 109.

[20] "Pour le pain, celui de Paris est grossier et compact; les délicats usent du pain de Gonesse, blanc, léger et fait avec du levain ..." Mongrédien, p. 92. Gonesse is a small town in the department of Seine et Oise.

[21] Max Lüthi, *Once Upon a Time — On the Nature of Fairy Tales,* trans. Lee Chadeayne and Paul Gottwald (New York: Fred. Ungar, 1970), p. 92.

> ... ils avaient approuvé les feux naissants qui s'allumaient dans leurs âmes: la parfaite beauté dont le ciel les avait doués, leur esprit, les grâces dont toutes leurs actions étaient accompagnées, faisaient souhaiter que leur union fût éternelle; mais ils la regardèrent d'un œil bien différent quand ils envisagèrent qu'elle était leur fille, et que le berger n'était sans doute qu'un malheureux ... (II, p. 45)

How convincing are these parents whose attitude changes when it comes down to their own home and their own daughter. This is an example of universal human nature at its best. This is the sort of reality that makes the reader able to accept her enchantments and believe her magic.

There are times when the author adds little explanations about the *merveilleux* in her tales. The best illustration of this comes in "Belle-Belle ou le Chevalier Fortuné" after the third daughter has helped the fairy shepherdess get her sheep out of the ditch.

> Car enfin, disait-elle, je ne lui étais pas nécessaire pour retirer son mouton; puisqu'un seul coup de sa baguette pourrait faire revenir un troupeau tout entier des antipodes, s'il y était tombé. J'ai été bien heureuse de me trouver si disposée à l'obliger; ce rien que j'ai fait pour elle est cause de tout ce qu'elle a fait pour moi; elle a connu mon cœur, et mes sentiments lui ont été agréables. (II, p. 153)

This is a familiar fairy tale motif — performing a service through desire to help, not for the benefit to be derived from the act. It is encountered more often with grateful animals than with grateful fairies. This may be the reason Mme. d'Aulnoy thought it needed an explanation. In "L'Oranger et l'abeille" Aimée steals the ogre's magic wand and escapes with her cousin Aimé. The ogre dons his seven-league boots and catches up with them. Then our *conteuse* explains:

> On s'étonnera qu'avec la baguette d'ivoire, ils n'allaient pas encore plus vite que lui: mais la belle princesse était bien neuve dans l'art de féerie. (I, p. 195)

Even a magic wand requires some know-how if it is to work properly! These insights satisfy our desire for logic within the framework of our imagination. It is unique. Those critics who claim that

Perrault provides a sense of the *merveilleux* without actually peopling his tales with fairies should not condemn Mme. d'Aulnoy's use of the *merveilleux* as being too obvious. Beneath the obvious there is a realism, as seen in the above examples, that turns her fairies into humans and her humans into fairies.

Another instance of her offering an explanation of her magic appears in "La Princesse Belle-Etoile et le Prince Chéri" where the three daughters have been granted a wish and have chosen the king, the prince and the admiral as their husbands. The engagements are arranged so quickly that the king is a little bewildered as he is invited in to eat.

> Quand le roi fut prêt à dîner, on vit descendre par la cheminée une table de sept couverts d'or, et tout ce qu'on peut imaginer de plus délicat pour faire un bon repas. Cependant le roi hésitait à manger, il craignait que l'on n'eût accommodé les viandes au sabbat; et cette manière de servir par la cheminée lui était un peu suspecte. (II, p. 238)

When the characters themselves are suspicious about the happenings in a tale, it adds a note of irony much like that of Perrault's tales. The striking part of this sort of irony is that it enhances the adult's enjoyment of the tale while not lessening the appeal to the child. It has often been pointed out that Mme. d'Aulnoy's tales were not written primarily for children, unless perhaps it was the children at court who would understand all of the allusions to court life. It seems a weak argument to say that only those who were cognizant of court affairs could appreciate her fairy tales. On the contrary, with all the interest evidenced in the happenings at Louis XIV's court, it would seem probable that her tales would fascinate doubly the curious who were not privileged to share in court matters. Delaporte quoted the *Mercure Galante* of July, 1698, as saying: "que les contes continuent d'estre en vogue, que les Fées à la mode, par Mme d***, sont du nombre de ceux qui ont le plus réussi." [22] The fact is that the public liked her first *contes de fées* so much that they demanded more.

---

22 Delaporte, p. 72.

One aspect of her work that is intriguing is her use of asides to the reader. This recalls the technique used by story tellers in the folk tradition of including some of their own thoughts or experiences in narrating their stories. It might be a simple comment as to a name used as in "L'Oiseau bleu." The enchanter visits the fairy, who asks him "Que me veut mon compère? . . . (c'est ainsi qu'ils se nomment tous)" (I, p. 68). She has already mentioned that enchanters and fairies had known each other for five or six hundred years and, during that time, performed many good and evil acts together. The addition of "mon compère" gives a familiarity to their relationship that renders their evil acts less frightening. Again in "La Princesse Printanière" the king calls his daughter "Ma petite brebiette (car il lui donnait toutes sortes de noms d'amitié)." These little asides or parenthetical comments create a sort of bond between the reader and the author, for the latter shows her understanding of human relationships.

Mme. d'Aulnoy's asides can be of a moral nature at times. After Princess Printanière runs away with Fanfarinet, she realizes that his hunger is overpowering his love.

> La princesse, affligée, courut dans le bois, déchirant ses beaux habits aux ronces, et sa peau blanche aux épines; elle était égratignée comme si elle avait joué avec des chats, (voilà ce que c'est d'aimer les garçons, il n'en arrive que des peines). (I, p. 126)

Printanière's experiences would serve as a warning to any young lady who might consider running off with her lover instead of performing her *devoir*. There is a sophisticated, worldly note at the end of this tale. Merlin's son wants to marry Printanière so "L'on n'eut garde de lui conter l'aventure de l'enlèvement, cela lui aurait peut-être donné quelques soupçons" (I, p. 132). There is a hint of La Fontaine here, for his *Contes* were known for their seeming lack of restraint. Mme. d'Aulnoy's works could never be called licentious because she is too proper, but from time to time she does suggest a certain worldly wisdom.

Montégut accused Mme. d'Aulnoy of being too moral. "Cette moralité si directe et si logique détruit toute illusion et toute impression du merveilleux." [23] Moral she was, along with many of her

---

[23] Montégut, p. 663.

contemporaries, but certainly not to the extent which Montégut suggests. If we take for an example one of her most popular tales, L'Oiseau bleu," we can prove that the moral does not destroy the *merveilleux,* but rather results from it. Had the young King Charmant who comes to court and falls in love with the pretty daughter, Florine, not been changed by the evil fairy Soussio into a bluebird, we would have no example of true love. The Yonec theme of the supernatural lover is continued and enlarged upon as the bluebird visits his lady love each night and woos her by caressing her with his wing. When the enchanter bargains for him to resume his human shape, it becomes the turn of the heroine to prove her love. She sets out to search for her bluebird. On the way she meets an old lady (fairy), who gives her four magic eggs. She uses these to trick Truitonne, the ugly sister, and win back her lover. It is the union of the enchanter and the old lady-fairy which overcomes the evil fairy Soussio so that true love can prevail. The moral is that one should marry for love. The *merveilleux* merely provided the tests to prove that their love was pure. In a later tale, also dealing with bird lovers — "Le Pigeon et la colombe" — the moral states that vicissitudes add to the pleasure of pure love. Hence the moral becomes a theme of her work carried by the motif of magic or *merveilleux.*

Mme. d'Aulnoy's tales, without the moral verse at the end, maintain all the magic and enchantment that a fairy tale could be expected to have. Her concluding moral is often threefold. It gives a brief résumé of the story, then it admonishes the present century for not exhibiting good sense or reason in the matter and finally, it offers an admonition or advice on human behavior. "La Grenouille bienfaisante" illustrates this type of moral.

> La reine que je viens de peindre,
> Au milieu des horreurs d'un infernal séjour,
> Pour ses jours n'avait rien à craindre;
> Pour elle l'amitié se joignit à l'amour.
> Grenouillette et le roi lui manquèrent leur zèle.
> Par de communs efforts.
> Malgré la Lionne cruelle,
> Ils surent l'arracher de ces funestes bords.
> Des époux si constants, des amis si sincères,
> Etaient du vieux temps de nos pères,
> Ils ne sont plus de ce temps-ci:

> Le siècle de féerie en à toute la gloire.
> Par le trait que je cite ici,
> De l'époque de mon histoire
> On peut être assez éclairci. (II, p. 75)

Not all of the morals make a direct reference to her own century or time, but it is often understood when not openly expressed. The moral verses add little to her *contes*. When critics refer to her morals as being the raison d'être of her tales, they undoubtedly are thinking of the rhymed verse at the end of each tale rather than the actual moral of the story. The latter is usually expressed in the last line or two of the rather lengthy verse. Had she limited herself to these few lines wherein the moral proper is stated, she would have received less criticism for her overly zealous morality. For a century that praised brevity, her tales were often too long and her morals too pointed.

There are many other elements of seventeenth-century life depicted in the tales. There are numerous references to food — most often to "dragées, sucre et confiture." The most complete listing of culinary treats appears in "Le Mouton." The golden-horned sheep leads the princess to his realm.

> Enfin elle découvrit tout d'un coup une vaste plaine émaillée de mille fleurs différentes, dont la bonne odeur surpassait toutes celles qu'elle avait jamais senties; une grosse rivière d'eau de fleurs d'oranges coulait autour, des fontaines de vin d'Espagne, de rossolis, d'hippocras et de mille autres sortes de liqueurs formaient des cascades et de petits ruisseaux charmants. Cette plaine était couvert d'arbres singuliers; il y avait des avenues tout entières de perdreaux, mieux piqués et mieux cuits que chez la Guérbois, et qui pendaient aux branches; il y avait d'autres allées de cailles et de lapereaux, de dindons, de poulets, de faisans et d'ortolans; en de certains endroits où l'air parassait plus obscur, il y pleuvait des bisques d'écrevisses, des soupes de santé, des foies gras, des ris de veau mis en ragoûts, des boudins, blancs, des saucissions, des tourtes, des pâtés, des confitures sèches et liquides, des louis d'or, des écus, des perles et des diamants. (I, p. 227)

Mongrédien mentions many of these same things as being generally in vogue in the seventeenth century.

A la fin du repas, il est d'usage de servir des vins très forts d'Italie et d'Espagne, "et on en boit hardiment", ainsi que des liqueurs alcoolisées: le ratafia, "espèce de kirsch fait avec des noyaux de pêche et d'abricots, très fort et d'un goût très agréable"; le rossolis, la fenouillette de l'île de Ré, assez semblable à notre anisette, le populo, dont le parfum violent est dû à un mélange d'esprit-de-vin, de sucre, de clou de girofle, de poivre, d'anis, de coriandre, d'ambre et de musc. [24]

The reference to "le ratafia" is especially interesting since one of Mme. d'Aulnoy's heroines, Babiole, falls into a bottle of it belonging to the fairies!

Several of the tales suggest a Spanish influence. Foulché-Delbosc and Jeanne Roche-Mazon have debated at length about whether Mme. d'Aulnoy did or did not actually go to Spain and whether she did or did not write her own *Relation du Voyage d'Espagne*. The fact remains that she was influenced by Spain, for she wrote her *Nouvelles espagnoles* and either compiled or wrote her own version of a *Relation du Voyage d'Espagne*. In her *Contes des fées* there are several allusions to Spanish customs. In "Gracieuse et Percinet" Grognon wants to make her entrance on horseback "parce qu'elle avait ouï dire que les reines d'Espagne faisaient ainsi la leur" (I, p. 12). The young prince, Torticoli, in "Le Rameau d'or" bears similarities to Calderon's Segismundo. He, too, is locked in a tower and he, too, has "la tête pleine d'imaginations" (I, p. 152). In fact, the whole tale of "Le Rameau d'or" is filled with the dream versus reality theme. In "La Chatte blanche" the cat queen and her young man are served a *medianoche* upon his return. Earlier, in the same story, before her metamorphosis she had married another young man with only her dog and her parakeet as witnesses. There is a similar situation in "A Trompeur, Trompeur et demi," one of the interpolated Spanish stories in Scarron's *Roman comique*. Since this is not a custom that we find often in French literature, it is probably a Spanish practice that Scarron and Mme. d'Aulnoy both borrowed. Another marriage custom often seen in Spanish Golden Age dramas is that of having the servants wed at the same time as the hero and heroine. In "La Biche au bois," Bécafique, the hero's loyal friend, asks for and wins Giroflée, the heroine's lady-in-waiting.

---

[24] Mongrédien, p. 93.

Mme. Roche-Mazon mentions three other Spanish traits in Mme. d'Aulnoy's *contes*. Mme. Roche-Mazon recalls the son of a Spanish grandee in love with the English ambassador's daughter in "Serpentin vert." She also finds a resemblance between the enchanted palace in "Le Rameau d'or" and the Escorial. Finally, she mentions the Spanish superstition that certain witchcraft could change a coach into an orange crate and the occupant into an orange tree as in "L'Oranger et l'abeille." [25]

Just as Cervantes [26] made reference to Book One of *Don Quixote* in his Book Two, so does Mme. d'Aulnoy refer to her own works. In "La Chatte blanche" she describes a wall that has the history of all the fairies since the creation of the world.

> ... Les fameuses aventures de Peau d'Ane, de Finette, de l'Oranger, de Gracieuse, de la Belle au bois dormant, de Serpentin vert, et de cent autres, n'y étaient pas oubliées. Il fut charmé d'y reconnaître le prince Lutin; car c'était son oncle à la mode de Bretagne. (II, p. 113)

A continuity is added to her stories when relationships such as these are established between characters in different stories and when references are made to other works. One of the most appealing allusions is when the Prince Constancio is metamorphosed into a pigeon and loses the power of speech. He says, bemoaning his fate, "Me voilà pigeon: encore si je pouvais parler, comme parla autrefois l'Oiseau Bleu (dont j'ai toute ma vie aimé le conte) ..." (II, p. 225). He finally gains his speech but chooses to remain a pigeon and dwell the rest of his days with his lady dove, free from the duties of court. There is mention of her entire second volume in "La Biche au bois." Désirée has been transformed into

---

[25] Roche-Mazon, p. 18.

[26] Melvin D. Palmer's article, "Madame d'Aulnoy and Cervantes," *Romance Notes*, XI (1970), 595-98, cites the following passage from her *Relation du Voyage d'Espagne* to prove that she knew and enjoyed Cervantes. ["J'y trovai entr'autres l'histoire de Dom Quichot, ce fameux Chevalier de la Manche, dans laquelle] la naïveté et la finesse des expressions, la force des proverbes et ce que les Espagnols appellent *el pico*, c'est-à-dire la pointe et la délicatesse de la Langue, paroissent tout autrement que les traductions que nous en voyons en nostre Langue." (Ed. by Raymond Foulché-Delbosc, Librairie Klincksieck, Paris, 1926, p. 523). The part in brackets was not cited by Palmer, but is included here for clarity.

a doe in the daytime and takes her human form at night. Her lady-in-waiting, Giroflée, comes to live with her in the woods and says, "J'irai dans la ville la plus proche acheter des livres pour vous divertir; nous lirons les Contes nouveaux que l'on a faits sur les fées ..." (II, p. 101). The interesting note here is that "La Biche au bois" refers to the *Contes nouveaux* of which it is an integral part. This leads us to ask why an author would include a reference to her own works. Is it an effort at winning over the audience (*captatio benevolentiae*) or is it perhaps a strong awareness of and satisfaction with her authorship?

If we recall that the reference in "La Chatte blanche" is to a history of famous fairies painted in color on a transparent porcelain wall, we might discover a clue as to why Mme. d'Aulnoy made mention of her own works. This is far from the only wall history in her tales. In the same *conte* there is a superb room decorated with the history of famous cats.

> On voyait autour l'histoire des plus fameux chats: Rodilardus pendu par les pieds au conseil des rats, Chat botté marquis de Carabas, le Chat qui écrit, la Chatte devenue femme, les sorciers devenus Chats, le sabbat et toutes ses cérémonies; enfin rien n'était plus singulier que ces tableaux. (II, p. 114)

Still another such history appears when the young prince performs his second task, that is, to find a piece of cloth that will go through the eye of a needle. The white cat puts the cloth inside five or six nuts, each smaller than the preceding. When finally it sees light,

> ... il en tira une pièce de toile de quatre cents aunes, si merveilleuse, que tous les oiseaux, les animaux et les poissons y étaient peints avec les arbres, les fruites et les plantes de la terre, les rochers, les raretés et les coquillages de la mer, le soleil, la lune, les étoiles, les astres et les planètes des cieux: il y avait encore le portrait des rois et autres souverains qui régnaient pour lors dans le monde celui de leurs femmes, de leurs maîtresses, de leur enfants et de tous leurs sujets, sans que le plus petit polisson y fût oublié. Chaucun dans son état faisait le personnage que lui convenait, et vêtu à la mode de son pays. (II, p. 124)

There are three histories in one tale — of fairies, of cats and of the world — each more wonderful than the preceding one. Yet, there are others. "La Biche au bois" has the fairies bring the baby princess a layette.

> Pour les dentelles, elles surpassaient encore ce que j'ai dit de la toile; toute l'histoire du monde y était réprésentée, soit à l'aiguille ou au fuseau. (II, p. 80)

"Le Dauphin" has a marvelous palace with the heroine's history represented on the wall of a large hall. Torticoli in "Le Rameau d'or" sees on the windows of the tower "des histoires qui étaient passées depuis plusieurs siècles" (I, p. 151), and among these he finds a portrait of himself. In "Gracieuse et Percinet" the princess is led by her prince charming to a crystal palace in the forest. There, she finds her own life history engraved on the wall. "... Les murs étaient de cristal de roche: elle y remarqua avec beaucoup d'étonnement que son histoire jusqu'à ce jour y était gravée" (I, p. 19). Here is a possible explanation of the histoires and probably of the references to her own works too. When Gracieuse says "à mesure que je fais une action et un geste, je le vois gravé," she expresses the idea that all of her actions and gestures are important enough to be engraved for posterity. Could these references to her own works and to the histories on the wall be a longing for immortality on Mme. d'Aulnoy's part? Are they both suggestive of a narcissism in Mme. d'Aulnoy? It appears so, especially since so many of the walls on which the histories are painted are crystal, transparent porcelain or window panes, all substances related to mirrors, which reflect the reality of the invisible world. It follows, then, that Mme. d'Aulnoy's fairy tales exhibit some baroque characteristics.

If we take Imbrie Buffum's listing of baroque traits as found in Braun's *Dictionary of French Literature,* we will discover that Mme. d'Aulnoy's tales display almost every characteristic of the baroque which he listed:

1. Moral purpose. Baroque literary works are generally animated by a moral intent, and often by a spirit of religious propaganda.
2. Devices of emphasis and exaggeration.
3. A taste for violence and horror.
4. Extremely concrete expression of abstract ideas.
5. Interest in theatricality and illusion.

6. Both with regard to content and form, a delight in contrast and surprise.
7. The stressing of movement and metamorphosis.
8. Despite all the foregoing — organic unity and the acceptance of life. [27]

Mme. d'Aulnoy has moral purpose beyond any doubt. As we saw earlier, Montégut even accused her of being too moral. Each tale has a clear moral stated in verse at the end of each tale as well as moral remarks and attitudes within the story itself. Storer has this to say of Mme. d'Aulnoy's moral purpose:

> Que la moralité soit en général la raison d'être de ces "bagatelles" de contes, c'est une preuve de l'immense influence du siècle sur cet auteur si peu moralisant dans sa vie particulière. [28]

Good examples of her use of emphasis would be the wall histories already referred to and perhaps the repeated use of metamorphoses and grateful animals. All of the *merveilleux* in her tales would fall under the rubric of exaggeration and under theatricality. There is almost a *deus ex machina* quality to some of the solutions in the tales. In "La Princesse Carpillon" a fairy defeats the blue centaur just as he is about to accept and eat the human sacrifice of our young hero. There are talking hands ("Le Rameau d'or"), talking carnations and cabbages ("Fortunée"), and even singing apples ("La Princesse Belle-Etoile et le Prince Chéri"). There are shipwrecks ("Le Dauphin"), substitute brides ("La Princesse Rosette"), giants ("Le Pigeon et la colombe"), ogres ("Finette Cendron"), dwarfs ("Le Nain jaune"), Dantesque monsters ("La Grenouille bienfaisante"); indeed there is so much magic that the reader begins to wonder what is real.

As for horror in Mme. d'Aulnoy's tales, there is little or none. However, in a passage quoted earlier from Storer, there was mention of "une veine de cruauté qui vous inquiète légèrement, lorsque vous pensez à la vie de l'auteur." [29] There are rather frequent allusions

---

[27] Sidney D. Braun, *Dictionary of French Literature* (New York: Philosophical Library, 1958), p. 17.
[28] Storer, p. 36.
[29] Storer, p. 41.

to biting and bleeding in the tales. Once a mouse bites the evil king's ear and it will not stop bleeding. The same mouse also eats the prince's only eye ("La Bonne petite souris"). Another time the frog takes a message to the captured queen's husband written in her blood ("La Grenouille bienfaisante"). In "Le Biche au bois" the enamored prince has to shoot the white doe in order to disenchant her. When the princess cuts the orange tree in "L'Oranger et l'abeille," it bleeds and his mate, the bee, has to go to Arabia for balm to cure him. One heroine is bitten by rats which cause her to bleed ("Fortunée"), and the brother seems to take delight in mistreating his sister. Another cruel character is Furibon, the king's son in "Le Prince Lutin." Furibon molests the fairy princess to such an extent that Léandre or Lutin has to cut off his head. A hint of cruelty is seen in the references to cannibalism in "La Princesse Rosette." The princess has run off to an island with a young man who becomes so hungry that he begins chasing her for his next meal. Fortunately, she has a magic stone which renders her invisible. If the fairy tale has a predilection for cruelty, it is due to its goal of making everything as sharp and distinct as possible. Therefore, the punishment must suit the crime. In "La Grenouille bienfaisante," the mistresses who cost the state blood are transformed into bloodsuckers and in "Serpentin vert," the heroine, Discrète, talks with those whom the fairies force to do penitence.

> . . . Elles firent des perroquets, des pies et des poules de celles qui parlaient trop; des pigeons, des serins et des petits chiens, des amants et des maîtresses; des singes de ceux qui contrefaisaient leurs amis; des cochons de certaines gens qui aimaient trop la bonne chère; des lions des personnes colères; enfin le nombre de ceux qu'elles mirent en pénitence fut si grand, que ce bois en est peuplé, de sorte que l'on y trouve des gens de toutes qualités et de toutes humeurs. (I, p. 333)

There is no better example of Mme. d'Aulnoy's expressing abstract idea in concrete terms than her moral verses. She rarely misses the opportunity to censure her century for lacking in fidelity or constancy.

> Des époux si constants, des amis si sincères,
> Etaient du vieux temps de nos pères,

Ils ne sont pas de ce temps-ci:
Le siècle de féerie en a toute la gloire.
("La Grenouille bienfaisante," p. 75)

Nor does she fail to proclaim the clemency of her king.

Apprenez qu'il est beau de pardonner l'offense
Après que l'on a su vaincre ses ennemis,
Et qu'on en peut tirer une juste vengence.
C'est ce que notre siècle admire dans Louis.
("La Princesse Rosette," I, p. 147)

She also extols true nobility.

Le seul mérite et la vertu
Font la véritable noblesse.
("Fortunée," I, p. 264)

Finally, she appeals to all of the senses in her use of color and smell, sound and sight, taste and touch throughout her vivid scenes.

What could be more theatrical than a fairy tale? Montégut described their dramaticality when he wrote of Mme. d'Aulnoy's tales:

> Ces contes sont une mascarade féerique, langage des grands seigneurs et des belles dames d'autrefois. Quelques-unes de ces fées à leur aurore avaient figuré peut-être dans la société de Mme de La Fayette ou de Julie d'Angennes, d'autres avaient sans doute leurs entrées chez la doyenne des fées du siècle, Mme de Maintenon. Tels qu'ils sont, ingénieux, spirituels, polis, souvent profonds, ce sont bien les contes de fées d'une société qui avait connu à son aurore les mascarades pastorales de la grande Mademoiselle, et qui devait connaître à son déclin les mascarades scientifiques et philosophiques de la duchesse du Maine en sa petite cour de Sceaux. Nous les recommandons aux faiseurs de ballets et de féeries dramatiques; ils y trouveront de jolis motifs de danses et de sujets de décors. [30]

Lüthi offers other dramatic characteristics of the fairy tale. He finds that reality is sublimated, but that feelings and relationships are

---

[30] Montégut, p. 670 (footnote).

externalized.[31] Hence, the fairy tale is all illusion sprinkled with realistic, even universal or cosmic, relationships. Tolkien, too, compares the consolation of the fairy tale to that of the drama.

> But the "consolation" of fairy-tales has another aspect than the imaginative satisfaction of ancient desires. Far more important is the Consolation of the Happy Ending. Almost I would venture to assert that all complete fairy-stories must have it. At least I would say that Tragedy is the true form of Drama, its highest function; but the opposite is true of Fairy-story. Since we do not appear to possess a word that expresses this opposite — I will call it *Eucatastrophe*. The *eucatastrophic* tale is the true form of fairy-tale, and its highest function.[32]

It may seem strange then that three of Mme. d'Aulnoy's tales have unhappy endings: her first, "L'île de la Félicité," "Le Mouton," and "Le Nain jaune." There are two possible explanations for her deviance here. First, and most likely, is that these three tales were to serve as a lesson or warning to those who would break promises or become too self-satisfied. Secondly, the moral proscribed any happy ending. Given the morals of the three tales, that is that there is no perfect happiness ("L'île de la félicité"), the high are subject to the same fortune as the low ("Le Mouton"), and you must not break your promises ("Le Nain jaune"); there is no way to please the public with a happy ending and present a moral lesson effectively. Other morals, such as the one in "La Bonne petite souris" which admonishes one to have a grateful heart and the one in "L'Oiseau bleu" which advocates that one marry for love, as well as the rest of the *contes,* follow the eucatastrophic development recommended by Tolkien.

The elements of contrast and surprise found in Mme. d'Aulnoy's tales are those extremes that are in most all fairy tales — good and evil, handsome and ugly, natural and supernatural, visible and invisible, real and unreal. What is unique is Mme. d'Aulnoy's use of good and bad fairies? Montégut stated very aptly this feature of her work:

---

31 Lüthi, pp. 51, 93.
32 Tolkien, p. 68.

Elle a très finement compris la puissance qu'exèrcent en notre pays ces forces toutes morales, subtiles comme l'esprit, mais invincibles comme lui, ces forces insaisissables, impondérables, qui s'appellent l'opinion, le préjugé, la faveur, la protection. C'est à juste titre que ces contes ingénieux portent pour titre: *les Enchantemens des bonnes et des mauvaises Fées.* Les princes et les princesses, les pages et les chevaliers de Mme d'Aulnoy sont comme prisonniers dans une geôle élastique; les influences sociales bonnes et mauvaises les enlacent de leurs réseaux subtils et pèsent sur eux d'un poids d'autant plus lourd qu'ils n'apercoivent pas le fardeau. C'est un tableau le plus souvent consolant, quelquefois comique, parfois aussi lamentable. Rien n'y peut égaler la douceur et la patience des bonnes fées, si ce n'est la perversité et la tenacité haineuse des mauvaises. [33]

The element of surprise is ever present too. When the hero, Alidor, of "Le Dauphin" sits down on a rock and an evil old fairy appears to reprimand him for resting on her rock, or when the seven *doués* (endowed ones) of "Belle-Belle ou la chevalier Fortuné" drink all the water from a pond and fill it with wine so that the dragon will drink it and become drunk enough that the hero can kill him, we are surprised and intrigued. These are but two examples of the many surprises and unusual experiences that greet the reader in the *contes*.

The tales are filled with action and movement. Most all of the heroes or heroines are peripatetic. They leave home on a quest, encounter myriad adventures and finally return home to marry and live happily ever after. Among their adventures is almost always a metamorphosis in Mme. d'Aulnoy's tales. Usually the hero or heroine is metamorphosed into an animal because of some evil or forgotten fairy's curse. These metamorphoses are the subject of another chapter where they are treated in detail.

Finally, the fairy tales express stoic acceptance of life in that they conquer time and inspire confidence. Max Lüthi explains it in this manner:

> The fairy tale conquers time by ignoring it. Part of the power which it has to delight the reader derives from this

---

[33] Montégut, p. 669.

triumph over time and the young and old people, but it does not portray the aging process. [34]

Since death is not ghostly in fairy tales and since some of the deceased reappear, as in "Le Prince Marcassin," there is acceptance of both life and death. Again, it is Lüthi who summarized the stoicism as well as several other baroque traits of the fairy tale in general and of Mme. d'Aulnoy's in particular.

> The fairy tale, however, not only inspires trust and confidence; it also provides a sharply defined image of man: isolated, yet capable of universal relationships. It is salutary that in our era, which has experienced the loss of individuality, nationalism, and impending nihilism, our children are presented with just such an image of man in the fairy tales they hear and absorb. This image is all the more effective for having proceeded naturally from the over-all style of the fairy tale. The fairy-tale technique — the sharp lines, the two-dimensional, sublimating portrayal we have so often observed as well as the capsuling of the individual episodes and motifs — this entire technique is isolating, and only for this reason can it interconnect all things so effortlessly. The image of man in the fairy tale, the figure of the hero, grows out of its over-all style: this gives it a persuasive power which cannot fail to impress even the realistically minded listener. [35]

Mme. d'Aulnoy is indeed a lady of her time. Her fairy tales exhibit classic and baroque qualities. Classic in the true sense of finding balance between reason and intuition, between moralizing and pleasing. Baroque, too, for many of the same reasons. The difference being that the baroque is polarized or one-sided. She shows *préciosité* in her language and attitudes and sentimentalism in her treatment of love. She is individualistic, for Storer refers to her as the innovator of the fairy tale in France; yet, at the same time, she is very much a part of her age. That she is ranked second to Perrault in the medium she chose to work in is no discredit. If Perrault is the master fairy storyteller, then she is, deservedly, the mistress.

---

[34] Lüthi, p. 44.
[35] Lüthi, p. 144.

CHAPTER IV

METAMORPHOSES AND GRATEFUL ANIMALS

THE SAME STATEMENT that Jean Giradoux made about La Fontaine
in his preface to the Gallimard Edition of *Les Fables* applies equally
well to Mme. d'Aulnoy. "...Les *Fables* de La Fontaine ne nous
montrent pas des hommes prenant des masques de bêtes, mais le
contraire."[1] These beasts endowed with human traits are characteristic of Mme. d'Aulnoy's personages.

Both La Fontaine and Mme. d'Aulnoy put the accent on the
human traits of their animals. Just as Babiole's heart "n'avait pas
été métamorphosé comme le reste de sa personne," so the other
animals retain some of their former humanness. In La Fontaine's
"Le Lion amoureux," a lion falls in love with a shepherdess and
asks for her hand in marriage. Because of his fierce claws and teeth,
they cannot refuse him, but they do take advantage of a weakness
— his love for the girl. They entreat him to let them clip his claws
and teeth so as not to frighten or harm his bride-to-be. He falls
into their trap and the dogs chase him away. Prudence goes out
the window when love comes in. Prince Marcassin is a boar who,
like La Fontaine's lion, wants to wed a young lady. Because of his
royal position, two sisters are forced to wed him, but both end in
tragedy — their death. Marcassin decides that his boarish instincts
would be better suited to the woods than to court. There, he wins
the third sister and regains his former body by fulfilling the fairy
prophecy of wedding three times. The moral is that it is better not
to know love than not to know wisdom. Both the lion and the boar

---

[1] Jean de La Fontaine, *Fables* (Paris: Gallimard, 1964), p. 16.

are foolish to think that lovely humans would want to marry them, yet they act in a human way as they let themselves be blinded by love. Marcassin, however, is bewitched by a fairy so that after fulfilling the prophecy, his body becomes human again as his heart and mind have been all the while. There are many similarities between La Fontaine and Mme. d'Aulnoy in their treatment of animals which we shall note throughout this chapter.

If we follow Stith Thompson's motif-index under Magic,[2] we shall discover that Mme. d'Aulnoy's metamorphoses or transformations run the gamut of the listings there, for almost all of her tales have some sort of metamorphosis, be it a permanent one such as that in "Le Pigeon et la colombe" or be it a simple disguise as that in "Belle-Belle ou le chevalier Fortuné." However, the index does offer a convenient cadre for organizing her tales of metamorphoses.

All but two ("La Belle aux cheveux d'or" and "La Princesse Rosette") of the twenty-five *contes* have some kind of transformation. Three of Mme. d'Aulnoy's stories would fall under Thompson's first transformation — man to different man. These are the same three that Krüger classified as being primarily pastoral. This is not surprising if we consider the popularity of the pastoral in court circles of the seventeenth century. If a king changes status, it is never to any mundane, intermediary bourgeois state, but rather to the other extreme of shepherd. This is one of the traits of fairy tale characters. They are either rich or poor, beautiful or ugly, noble or peasant, but never in between. The pastoral life was highly idealized from *L'Astrée* on through the entire century. The three *contes* with pastoral transformations are "La Princesse Carpillon," in which the king, the hero and the heroine all become shepherds, thus changing from a high social status to a lower one; "Le Rameau d'or," in which the extremely ugly hero and heroine are transformed into beautiful bodies through their own virtue and then into shepherds; and "Le Pigeon et la colombe," in which the heroine-princess is reduced to a lowly shepherdess to escape a giant. A unique aspect of this tale is that the prince is transformed through love into a pigeon and his princess becomes a dove. They elect to

---

[2] Thompson, p. 30. The following are listed: man to different man, man to animal, man to object, animal to person, and other forms of transformation.

keep their bird forms eternally so that their love can flourish free from worldly cares.

A fourth tale in this category shows an entirely different transformation. Instead of changing social status, Fanfarinet, of "La Princesse Printanière," becomes cannibalistic. A psychological analysis of this tale would interpret the desire to eat his mistress as a sexual yearning and the heroine's invisibility as a repression of the same desire. It adds a plausible explanation, especially when reinforced by other sexual symbols such as the queen's crown with jewels and the king's dagger which the lovers took with them as they escaped. Cannibalism is sometimes equated with the idea of separation of body and soul. It occurred to the primitive mind that if the soul wanted to return to the body, it would be simpler to eat the body so that the survivor could acquire the powers of the dead. Perhaps Mme. d'Aulnoy's salon coterie read deeper or more worldly meanings into the *contes* as they listened to them, but most indications lead us to believe that she wrote them to entertain or to please. For that, the literal, surface level of meaning is sufficient. It is to her credit that the tales lend themselves to so many different kinds of interpretation, for it makes them all the more valuable in that whosoever reads them can derive some profit or pleasure from them.

By far the largest number of Mme. d'Aulnoy's fairy tales involve the transformation of man to animal. Naturally, there is some overlapping, as in "Le Rameau d'or" or "Le Pigeon et la colombe" where there are transformations of man to different man and from man to animal. For the most part, the other eight tales with animal transformations ("L'Oiseau bleu," "Le Mouton," "Babiole," "Serpentin vert," "La Biche au bois," "La Chatte blanche," "Le Dauphin," and "Le Prince Marcassin") relate how the hero or heroine is changed into an animal by a fairy curse or enchantment. Yearsley found that

> This union of man and the lower animals is in harmony with primitive thought, and is traceable to the stage of Naturism and Animism. But the imputation of the characteristics of man to brutes and inanimate things is more than primitive — it is the perpetually recurring will-o'-the-wisp of our imagination. When man's essential distinction came to be recognized by widening knowledge, the ideas

of metempsychosis and later of enchantment grew up as a
support for the conviction that still haunts us. Possibly
enchantment is a later gloss on earlier, bolder Animism.[3]

This is an interesting facet of the metamorphoses, that is that man
is essentially one with the animals. There are numerous references
to man's resemblance to animals in the *contes,* often to man's
disadvantage. When Prince Marcassin asks the first sister to marry
him, he adds, "J'avoue que je ne suis pas beau; mais on dit que
tous les hommes ont quelque ressemblance avec des animaux" (II,
p. 296). After the second sister tries to kill him, he rationalizes, "Je
suis homme sous la figure d'une bête. Combien y a-t-il de bêtes
sous la figure d'hommes!" (II, p. 305). Finally, the third sister is
tricked into coming with him into his cave. She reproaches him for
not keeping his promise to let her leave. Marcassin's retort shows
clearly that the author's sympathy is with the animal side of man.

> Il faut bien, lui dit-il en souriant à la marcassine, qu'il y
> ait un peu de l'homme mêlé avec le sanglier, le défaut de
> parole que vous me reprochez, cette petite finesse où je
> ménage mes intérêts, c'est justement l'homme qui agit; car
> pour parler sans façon, les animaux ont plus d'honneur
> entre eux que les hommes. (II, pp. 311-12)

In "Le Dauphin," when Alidor asks the dolphin why the evil
fairy Grognette is against him when he has done nothing to dis-
please her, the dolphin explains, "Quoi! vous êtes homme, et vous
vous étonnez de l'injustice des hommes?" (II, p. 231). La Fontaine,
too, protested man's injustice. Given the choice between man and
animal, he opted for animal, as did Mme. d'Aulnoy. Throughout the
tales, the reader feels that the author has a special understanding
of animals. They are more memorable characters and certainly more
noble than a father who permits a jealous stepmother to have full
sway over a stepdaughter and sits idly by while the daughter suffers
all manner of punishment ("Gracieuse et Percinet"), or a mother
who gives her own daughter to the fairies for some of their magic
fruit ("La Chatte blanche") or even parents who abandon their
children ("Finette Cendron"). C. S. Lewis' comment on these "other

---

[3] Macleod Yearsley, *The Folklore of Fairy-Tale* (London: Watts & Co.,
1924), pp. 51-52.

than human" characters adds a dimension of depth to the fairy tale as a genre.

> ... The presence of beings other than humans which yet behave, in varying degrees, humanly: the giants and dwarfs and talking beasts. I believe these to be at least (for they may have other sources of power and beauty) an admirable hieroglyphic which conveys psychology, types of character, more briefly than novelistic presentation and to the readers whom novelistic presentation could not reach. [4]

Certainly it is more obvious to a child or even to the adult reader of fairy tales when the characters are clearly defined and unchanging. As Cirlot pointed out in his *Dictionary of Symbols,*

> ... while man is an equivocal "Masked" or complex being, the animal is univocal, for its positive or negative qualities remain ever constant. [5]

The passages that describe the actual metamorphosis are among the most appealing of Mme. d'Aulnoy's work. The vivid descriptions enhance the transformation by their exactitude of details or by their touches of irony and humor. The former may be seen in "L'Oiseau bleu" when the fairy Soussio condemns Prince Charmant to seven years of penance as a bluebird for not wedding her ugly godchild, Truitonne.

> En même temps le roi change de figure: ses bras se couvrent de plumes et forment des ailes; ses jambes et ses pieds deviennent noirs et menus; il lui croit des ongles crochus; son corps s'apetisse; il est tout garni de longues plumes fines et déliées de bleu céleste; ses yeux s'arrondissent et brillent comme des soleils; son nez n'est plus qu'un bec d'ivoire; il s'élève sur sa tête une aigrette blanche qui forme une couronne; il chante à ravir et parle de même. (I, p. 53)

It is as if we were present as we observe, step by step, the gradual shift of arms to wings, legs to claws, skin to blue feathers, nose to

---

[4] C. S. Lewis, *Of Other Worlds, Essays and Stories,* ed. by Walter Hooper (New York: Harcourt, Brace & World, 1966), p. 27.
[5] J. E. Cirlot, *A Dictionary of Symbols,* trans. Jack Sage (New York: Philosophical Library, 1962), p. 10.

bill, hair to tuft and a voice that begins to sing like a bird. Yet, the prince does not lose the ability to speak. The talking beast is a phenomenon that has intrigued man from primitive times to the Christian era and even up to modern times with the popularity of Walt Disney and his menagerie of talking animals. Yearsley finds that these stories about animals and their talk hark back to pre-historic sources such as the Buddhist *Jatakas* and the ancient Persian Fables of Bidpai which influenced Aesop's fables. He notes that

> ... the talking animals of all folk-tales descend from an age when it was one of the commonplaces of thought and belief that animals did and could talk, and were, in effect, nothing but men and women in animal shape. [6]

Mme. d'Aulnoy certainly follows tradition in her view of the human quality of animals. She shows a great understanding of animal and human psychology. Without saying it, she makes the reader feel what the Basque peasants often said as they began their stories: "This happened, sir, in the time when all animals and all things could speak." [7] Such is the power of her magic.

In "Le Mouton" the reader is not present for the metamorphosis, for the hero is already a sheep when the heroine first encounters him. However, as he relates his own story to her, he tells how the cruel fairy, Ragotte, took her revenge on him for not returning her passion for him.

> Aussitôt elle me toucha de sa baguette, et je me trouvai métamorphosé comme vous voyez. Je ne perdis point l'usage de la parole, ni les sentiments de douleur que je devais à mon état. (I, p. 230)

Thus, Mme. d'Aulnoy emphasizes those human traits, such as speech and emotions, that normally distinguish man from animal. She seems to sense intuitively which animal characteristics and which human traits to combine in order to realize that perfect blend of believability. Edmond Pilon appreciated the originality of her transformations when he wrote: "Ces métamorphoses ont souvent inspiré — surtout au dix-septième siècle — des contes d'une bigarrure des plus ingé-

---

[6] Yearsley, p. 52.
[7] Yearsley, p. 52.

nieuses." [8] He mentioned as an example the strange happenings in Mme. d'Aulnoy's "Le Dauphin." Doubtless, he had reference to Alidor's transformation into a canary so he can sleep near the lady he loves. The canary, known as Biby, summons enough courage to ask the king and queen for their daughter in marriage. He explains that he is the sovereign of the Canary Islands and that his subjects supply him with enough bugs and worms so that the princess "en pourra manger tout son saoul" (II, p. 328). He also promises to provide her with entertainment, for he has some relatives who are nightingales. Lastly, he tells his future in-laws that it will be easy to keep in touch with their daughter because of his "courriers volants." The king and queen treat the request as a joke and agree to it if Livorette, their daughter, desires it. All go along with the mockery until it is discovered that Livorette is expecting! Alidor's metamorphosis differs from some of the others in that he can become a canary when it suits him or keep his own form. In addition, his transformation is bestowed on him by a friend, the dolphin, who favored Alidor out of gratitude for having saved his life earlier.

The dolphin is one of several grateful animals in Mme. d'Aulnoy's *contes*. Throughout folklore there are tales of grateful beasts. These animals often perform impossible tasks for the person who befriends him. It is essential that the person help the animal with no thought of recompense or the magic will not work. One must be benevolent naturally with no thought of self gain for the animal to reciprocate. Such is the case in "La Belle aux cheveux d'or" where the hero saves three animals: one from the sea, a carp; one from the air, a crow; and one from the night, an owl. All are able to help him in the tasks imposed on him later by the princess. The carp finds the ring that was lost in the water, the crow plucks out the giant's eye and the owl goes to the dark cave to get the magic water. This element of harmonious fit in the fairy tale is what adds to the sense of consolation that the reader derives from fairy tales. Max Lüthi confirmed this view when he wrote:

> The fairy tale portrays, in a wider sense than is generally realized, a harmonious world. The confidence from which

---

[8] Edmond Pilon, *Bonnes Fées d'antan* (Paris: E. Santot et Cie., Bibliothèque Internationale d'Edition, 1909), p. 10.

it flows is transmitted to both those who tell it and those
who hear it. . . . It gives not only pleasure, it gives form
and inspiration; and we can readily believe the report of
a north German storyteller that a soothing and healing
power can emanate from fairy tales when told to sick
people in hospitals. Every fairy tale is, in its own way,
something of a dragon slayer.[9]

The satisfaction brought about by this harmony within the tale and
by what Tolkien called the eucatastrophic ending console the reader
or the hearer by offering symbolic experiences rather than realistic
ones.

In "Le Pigeon et la colombe" there are grateful animals, but
here it is rather a minor element of the story. The heroine saves
the other animals as well as her sheep when she cuts them out of
the giant's bag. Since it is night, they lead her out of the woods
since she cannot see. The grateful animal in "La Bonne petite
souris" and in "La Grenouille bienfaisante" is a fairy. In both
instances the queens who are captured are expecting a child. One
befriends a mouse and the other a frog. Later the animals render a
service to their queens and finally reveal that they are fairies. Pilon
alluded to the fact that they, too, could change form.

Elles-mêmes avaient le secret de se rendre invisibles et de
changer de formes autant de fois qu'elles voulaient.[10]

In "La Princesse Belle-Etoile et le Prince Chéri" a good fairy
changes into a siren, then a dove to serve the heroine. Another
fairy who becomes a serpent every hundred years is Gentille in "Le
Prince Lutin." It is the Mélusine[11] motif coupled with other themes,

---

9 Lüthi, p. 57.
10 Pilon, p. 9.
11 The *Roman de Mélusine* was written by Jean d'Arras in 1480. Three
daughters of the fairy Pressine try to punish their father, the King of Albany.
For this reason, their mother punishes them. Since Mélusine is most respon-
sible, her punishment is worse. Every Saturday her body becomes a serpent
from the waist down. If a young man will agree to wed her and never see
her on this unlucky day, she will be forever happy. Otherwise, she will be
condemned to keep a serpent's body until Judgment Day. She weds, but the
husband's curiosity wins out and he spies on her. She becomes a serpent
forever and all of their children bear some mark of her infamy. She is asso-
ciated with the castle of Lusignan. It is said that she appears to all of the

thereby causing the story to take a different turn. This mixing of motifs from various tales is characteristic of Mme d'Aulnoy. Who else would ever have dreamed of combining themes from "Le Petit Poucet," "Cendrillon," and "Hansel and Gretel" into one story as she does in her "Finette Cendron"? Another theme from "Le Petit Poucet" — the clever exchange of the little ogres' crowns to a human head at night so that the ogre eats his own child in lieu of the stranger — is saved for "L'Oranger et l'abeille." Mme. d'Aulnoy's shuffling of motifs is a trait that suggests that she did not follow the simplicity of oral tradition. Part of her artistry stems from the original manner in which she fuses different motifs together. The irony is that this is exactly the same way that tales grew and were modified in oral tradition. Still, the four fairies mentioned here are the only ones that change into animal forms in Mme. d'Aulnoy's *contes*. The others might become old women ("La Biche au bois," "L'Oiseau bleu," "Le Rameau d'or," and "Belle-Belle ou le Chevalier Fortuné") in order to carry out their good or evil deeds, but mainly Mme. d'Aulnoy's fairies cause transformations in humans.

In the four remaining tales of transformation from man to animal ("Serpentin vert," "Babiole," "La Chatte blanche" and "La Biche au bois"), the metamorphoses are due to a fairy's revenge on the human for neglecting or slighting her. In these tales the disenchantment is achieved by rather ingenious means. Serpentin vert is "déserpentiné" by Laideronnette's love as evidenced from her performance of tasks in his behalf. Babiole becomes human by eating an olive from a box that emits a special perfume that transforms her. The doe in "La Biche au bois" is shot in the leg by her prince and never becomes a doe again. Whether it is the penetration of the lover's arrow into her flesh or the flowing of blood that causes the transformation is unimportant, for the rightful lovers are together and a happy ending is in sight. [12] Lastly, the white cat ("La Chatte

---

descendants on the day of their death. Efforts have been made to establish her historicity by identifying her with numerous noble women.

[12] In any event, the reader is made aware that the real disenchantment came about through love as in Marie de France's lay, "Guigemar," when the white doe he wounded predicted how Guigemar's own wound would be healed.

> "Ja mais n'aies tu medecine,
> Ne par herbe, ne par racine,
> Ne par mire, ne par poison
> N'avras tu ja mais guarison

blanche") resumes her human body when a young prince cuts off her head and tail and throws them in a fire.

Mme. d'Aulnoy offers no transformations of man to object unless it would be the several changes Aimée makes with her stolen magic wand in "L'Oranger et l'abeille." Aimée and her cousin-lover, Aimé, are trying to escape from the ogres who raised her. They are on a camel, and the ogre overtakes them in his seven-league boots, so Aimée uses the ivory wand to transform them into some form the ogre will not recognize. For the first metamorphosis, she proceeds in the following manner:

> Je souhaite, dit-elle, au nom de la royale fée Trusio, que notre chameau devienne un étang, que le prince soit un bateau, et moi une vieille batelière qui le conduirai. (I, pp. 195-96)

The second metamorphosis is conducted in a similar fashion:

> Je souhaite, dit-elle, au nom de la royale fée Trusio, que le prince soit métamorphosé en portrait, le chameau en pilier, et moi en nain. (I, p. 192)

The third and final metamorphosis is as follows:

> Je souhaite, au nom de la royale fée Trusio, que le chameau soit une caisse, que mon cher prince devienne un bel oranger, et que métamorphosée en abeille, je vole autour de lui. (I, p. 199)

This last transformation gave the title to the tale because the wand is stolen and they have to remain in this form until Princess Linda solicits the aid of Trusio, who changes them into Aimée and Aimé. Jeanne Roche-Mazon mentioned a Spanish superstition that certain witchcraft could change a coach into an orange crate and the occupant into an orange tree as a possible influence on or source of this *conte*. Wherever Mme. d'Aulnoy received her inspiration, it is

---

De la plaie qu'as en la cuisse,
Decique cele te garisse,
Qui sofferra por teue amor . . ."

The Lays of Marie de France, ed. by Robert White Linker (Chapel Hill: University of North Carolina Press, 1947), p. 4.

her own original reworking of superstitions or other commonplaces of folklore that captivates the modern reader as well as the seventeenth-century audience. It does seem strange at first that the prince is changed into a boat, a painting and an orange tree — all objects, but it must be remembered that Aimée is the clever one who knows how to trick the ogres and she keeps herself in a form to handle any situation which might arise.

This female dominance is found all through Mme. d'Aulnoy's tales. Even in the *contes* with titles bearing the hero's name, it is the heroine who motivates the action. In "Le Mouton," for example, the sheep is of secondary importance, for the main incident is of the Joseph type, that is the dream of future greatness with the parent serving the child and his attempt to get rid of the youth. The child in Mme. d'Aulnoy's story is the youngest of three sisters. When she returns for the second sister's wedding and the prophecy is fulfilled, the sheep is no longer needed so he dies of grief outside the palace gate. If we follow only the principal happening, there is the usual fairy tale happy ending. It appears that the secondary element dealing with the sheep was added so that the tale would have a moral, for without a moral no tale was complete in the seventeenth century. Just at the moment when the princess believes she has been reunited with her father and all is well, she learn of the loss of her dear sheep and the moral follows immediately:

> Les plus élevées sont sujettes, comme les autres, aux coups de la fortune, et que souvent elles éprouvent les plus grands malheurs dans le moment où elles se croient au comble de leurs souhaits. (I, p. 235)

The secondary motif might be seen as an obstacle to the fruition of the primary one. The sheep would have liked to prevent her from going back to the wedding because "un pressentiment secret lui annonçait son malheur" (I, p. 233). In spite of this obstacle, she returns to her father and the fulfillment of the prophecy.

The other two tales that purportedly have unhappy endings are "Le Nain jaune" and "La Princesse Félicité et le Prince Adolphe." The latter is sometimes referred to as "L'Ile de la Félicité" and is more of an allegory than a fairy tale. Man searches for happiness and finds it, but it does not last forever. Had Prince Adolphe not been of the seventeenth century so that he felt compelled to leave his mistress and perform his duty in order to maintain his *vertu* and his *gloire,* then his happiness might have endured forever.

The real heroine of "Le Nain jaune" is Toute-Belle. She breaks her promise to the ugly dwarf and is punished. She perishes just after her lover is killed and the siren transforms them into palm trees with branches intertwining to conserve their love forever. Thus, their love is immortalized just as Pyramus and Thisbe's was by a tree which becomes the memorial of their love. Since they can not be joined in life, they will be forever joined in death. It is the heroine who made the decision to die with her lover rather than yield to the dwarf.

The dominance of female characters often shows great insight into feminine psychology. Gracieuse, for example, prefers to suffer a whipping than to call Percinet to help her in her state of disarray.

> En toute autre détresse, Gracieuse aurait souhaité le beau Percinet; mais se voyant presque nue, elle était trop modeste pour vouloir qu'un prince en fût témoin. (I, p. 15)

Motherly instincts are present too. Even Babiole's mother feels compassion for the little monster whom she bore and believed to be dead.

> Mais au fond, continuait-elle, c'est ma fille, c'est mon sang, c'est moi qui lui ai attiré l'indignation de la méchante Fanferluche. (I, p. 279)

Even certain fairies show devotion and attachment to the humans they endow in Mme. d'Aulnoy's stories. Tulipe in "La Biche au bois" is filled with motherly caution concerning her young protégée whom an evil fairy has cursed with bad luck if she should see daylight before age fifteen.

> Tulipe l'aimait davantage, et recommandait plus soigneusement à la reine de ne lui pas laisser voir le jour avant qu'elle eût quinze ans. (II, p. 83)

Yet this faithful fairy is not content with a mere warning. She becomes an old lady in whose cabin Princess Désirée and her handmaiden dwell while the former is under metamorphosis. Finally, after the disenchantment, she assures Désirée's future happiness:

La fée Tulipe, qui était encore plus libérale que ses sœurs, lui donna quatre mines d'or dans les Indes, afin que son mari n'eût pas l'avantage de se dire plus riche qu'elle. (II, p. 110)

Not only is she protective, she is practical in matters that only female perception or intuition can foresee. If the "l'homme et l'œuvre" method were applied to her, it would doubtless attribute this concern for the wife's having money in her own right to Mme. d'Aulnoy's own personal life. Her differences with Baron d'Aulnoy were, indeed, financial, and if there were many references in her works to the importance of the wife's being independently wealthy, then we might concur, but this seems to be the only reference.

Returning to Thompson's classifications, we find three tales that might be listed under the transformation from man to plant. We have already alluded to the metamorphosis of Aimé into an orange tree in "L'Oranger et l'abeille" and the eternal metamorphosis of the lovers into palm trees at the end of "Le Nain jaune." Finally, in "Fortunée" the young prince is transformed into a carnation. As his mother, la Reine des bois, explains his metamorphosis, it is quite logical. Having magic gifts, she entreats the winds to substitute her own baby son for her sister's daughter so that her sister can provide her husband with the heir he has demanded. The winds place the infant in a flower bed while searching for the queen. An enemy fairy transforms the son into a carnation since he is already in a flower bed. Here is a perfect example of the Cartesianism often attributed to French fairies. Their metamorphoses are logical and even natural. Yearsley referred to these transformations as the logical sequence of Animism and went on to equate them to the changes in nature.

> Another point to be remembered is that a belief in transformation receives apparent confirmation in the wonderful changes which are constantly seen in nature. The emergence of the chick from the egg, the metamorphosis of the caterpillar into the chrysalis and of the chrysalis into the butterfly, of the dragon-fly from its unprepossessing, dirty-looking larva, or of the acorn into the tiny seedling oak, all lend themselves to the human predilection for the marvelous. Such natural phenomena make the idea of an an-

imal turning into a man, a tree, or a stone, or *vice-versa,* easy to understand. [13]

Mme. d'Aulnoy's transformations do seem natural. Désirée, so pure and full of grace, becomes a demure, white doe. Most of the female transformations are into white animals, which might symbolize their purity — the white cat ("La Chatte blanche") and the white dove ("Le Pigeon et la colombe"). The vivacious and playful Babiole, whose name indicates her little value to her family, is rightfully a monkey, for she is capricious. Edith Cumings, too, mentioned the uniqueness of French transformations.

> This parallelism to nature in causing metamorphoses which remain within reasonable limits is in keeping with French restraint. [14]

As for the male metamorphoses, some of them are pragmatic. The choice of a pigeon ("Le Pigeon et la colombe") is imperative so that he can fly to the tower with the ring that will turn the captured princess into a dove and permit her to escape. The green serpent ("Serpentin vert") frightens Laideronnette more than death by his ugly appearance. The fairy he has spurned has changed him from the handsomest to the ugliest of creatures. Hence, his punishment is to be spurned by all women.

Cirlot associates metamorphosis with the concept of Inversion.

> . . . All opposites are for an instant fused together and then inverted. What is constructive turns to destruction; love turns to hate; evil to good; unhappiness to happiness; martyrdom to ecstasy. Corresponding to this inner inversion of a process is an outer inversion of the symbol pertaining to it. [15]

This tenet leads to all kinds of suppositions about the metamorphoses or inversions in Mme. d'Aulnoy's tales. First of all, as was pointed out earlier, everything is clearly delineated. Black is black and white is white. A fairy is good (Tulipe in "La Biche au bois")

---

[13] Yearsley, p. 59.

[14] Edith Cumings, "The Literary Development of the Romantic Fairy Tale in France" (Unpubl. diss., Bryn Mawr, 1934), p. 30.

[15] Cirlot, p. 150.

or evil (Magotine in "Serpentin vert"). A child is extremely beautiful (Toute-Belle in "Le Nain jaune") or terribly ugly (Laideronnette in "Serpentin vert"). A youth is exceptionally clever (Finette) or impossibly stupid (Truitonne in "L'Oiseau bleu"). One senses that the metamorphoses actually reverse the outward symbol while the inner being is undergoing the opposite process. Torticoli in "Le Rameau d'or" becomes physically handsome because of the inner goodness of his soul. The same is true of Toute-Belle in "Le Nain jaune." From a vain, proud, indifferent beauty, she is changed into a self-sacrificing, ever-faithful Juliet as she falls over the dead body of her Romeo. The outward sign of her new-found fidelity is their metamorphosis into palm trees.

> Ces deux corps si parfaits devinrent deux beaux arbres, conservant toujours un amour fidèle l'un pour l'autre, ils se caressent de leurs branches entrelacées, et immortalisent leurs feux par leur tendre union. (I, p. 310)

Mme. d'Aulnoy's inversions, then, may be an effort toward counterbalancing opposites such as good and evil, ugly and beautiful, life and death. Borgerhoff's premise about French classicism was that reason and freedom had to live in tension and that the real secret was that classic balance which never allowed either to reach a definitive form.[16] The duality of the metamorphoses maintains this kind of paradox between man's two natures, that is, the spiritual and the physical, the positive and the negative, or even the benefic and the malefic. Since most of Mme. d'Aulnoy's tales show some kind of metamorphosis, it is obviously one of her most important motifs and it carries the theme of the mutability of all things, for everything is in a constant state of flux in the twenty-five *contes*.

Those transformations which will be discussed next under the rubric of miscellaneous transformations differ from Thompson's index in that one area treated here would fall under what the index refers to as change of sex, but the present writer prefers to deal with it as disguise. The other area included arbitrarily is invisibility which, as interpreted here, involves a sort of miscellaneous metamorphosis, but could be listed in several places in the Thompson

---

[16] E. B. O. Borgerhoff, *The Freedom of French Classicism* (New York: Russell and Russell, 1968), pp. 239-41.

classification. There is only one of Mme. d'Aulnoy's tales that is constructed around a disguise and that is "Belle-Belle ou le chevalier Fortuné." According to Stith Thompson, it is a story developed by literary writers of the seventeenth and eighteenth centuries, which had been collected in several countries from oral raconteurs. [17] It is especially interesting, not only because of the daughter disguised as a warrior, but for her extraordinary companions collected along the way. As all of the animals in "La Belle aux cheveux d'or" were able to serve the hero later so all of the companions are necessary to the successful carrying out of the tasks imposed on Fortuné by the queen. It is the third and youngest sister who is able to help the old lady, whose sheep is in the ditch, and pass undetected to fulfill her family's duty to the king. Without this act, there would be no magic horse to advise her in selecting the extraordinary companions (doués) who would help her in all of her tasks. The other two sisters do not possess the rare virtue known as concern for others which would have enabled either of them to achieve their disguise and destiny. Is it just because it is a commonplace of folklore that the youngest is able to succeed where her elder sisters have failed or does it hark back to the primitive idea of the matriarchal society where the youngest is allotted a special connection to the hearth? By extension the youngest is specially endowed — cleverest as Finette Cendron, most honest as Merveilleuse in "Le Mouton," most humane as Belle-Belle, most forgiving as Blondine in "La Princesse Belle-Etoile et le Prince Cheri," or wisest as the youngest sister in "Le Prince Marcassin." Madame d'Aulnoy's fairy tales possess many of the commonplaces of the folktale, but we can only surmise what her intention is. She claimed that her primary goal was the same as La Fontaine's as stated in his preface to Les Amours de Psyché et Cupidon:

> Mon but principal est toujours de plaire: pour en venir
> là, je considère le goût du siècle. Or, après plusieurs ex-
> périences, il m'a semblé que ce goût se porte au galant et
> à la plaisanterie: non que l'on méprise les passions, ...
> mais dans un conte comme celui-ci, qui est plein de mer-

---

[17] Stith Thompson, The Folktale (New York: Dryden, 1946), p. 55.

veilleux accompagné de badineries, et propre à amuser des enfants, il a fallu badiner depuis le commencement jusqu'à la fin: il a fallu chercher du galant et de la plaisanterie. [18]

Please she did and what better choice could she have made than her own embellishments of tales from popular tradition?

The tales with invisible heroes are "Gracieuse et Percinet," "Le Prince Lutin," "La Princesse Printanière," and "La Princesse Félicité et le Prince Adolphe." All but "La Princesse Printanière" use their magic invisibility as a means of being near and winning the one they love. Percinet is the hero and also the helper since he was born with the "don de féerie" whereby he can perform many impossible tasks and make himself invisible. He comes to help Gracieuse through the misfortunes of a wicked stepmother who is as ugly as Gracieuse is pretty and as wicked as Percinet is good. Grognon, the stepmother, with the help of a fary, imposes task after task on Gracieuse. Percinet is ever ready to come to her rescue, although she continues to refuse to marry him lest he have "l'humeur légère des autres hommes, qui changent quand ils sont certains d'être aimés" (I, p. 28).

"Le Prince Lutin" is an interesting character who gains his invisibility as a gift awarded to him by a grateful fairy. Her destiny is to become a serpent for one week every hundred years and after Léandre saves her from a gardener, she makes him a "lutin." Since he has no idea what good it will do him to become a "lutin," he asks her and she replies:

> Vous êtes invisible quand il vous plaît; vous traversez en un instant le vaste espace de l'univers; vous vous élevez sans avoir des ailes; vous allez au fond de la terre sans être mort; vous pénétrez les abîmes de la mer sans vous noyer; vous entrez partout, quoique les fenêtres et les portes soient fermées; et, dès que vous le jugez à propos, vous vous laissez voir sous votre forme naturelle. (I, p. 84)

The "lutin" or sprite is mischievous. One of his first acts is to return to the palace and play a trick on Furibon, the devilish, ugly

---

[18] Cited by Kurt Krüger, p. 76. Also see La Fontaine, *Œuvres complètes,* ed. by Jean Marmier (Paris: Seuil, 1965), p. 404.

prince who mistreated him earlier. Later, he wins a fairy princess through his spritely invisibility.

Prince Adolphe becomes invisible by wearing a green coat that the wind, Zéphire, gives him so he can accompany him to the "île de la Félicité." There, he hopes to meet the lovely princess whom Zéphire told him so much about. He decides to enter the palace in a basket that a maiden lowers to the gardener to be filled with flowers. Mme. d'Aulnoy adds a clever aside to the reader concerning the details of his invisibility and his entrance to the palace.

> Il faut croire que le Manteau vert qui pouvoit le rendre invisible pouvoit aussi le rendre fort léger, sans cette circonstance il seroit difficile de le faire arriver jusques à la fenêtre aussi heureusement qu'il y arriva. [19]

This reference to a physical detail when dealing with a fantasy such as invisibility does not detract from the imaginative quality of the tale; rather it enhances it by adding just a trace of realistic doubt. The tales are filled with just such clever turns of thought that greatly delight the unsuspecting reader or listener.

Princess Printanière becomes invisible only once through the magic stone she took from her mother when she fled the palace with Fanfarinet, her lover. Fanfarinet wants to devour her so she makes herself invisible and kills him. A possible psychological interpretation of this act was discussed earlier. [20]

One last transformation that should be mentioned is the name change that accompanies many of the inner transformations. In fact, the entire sphere of names in fairy tales is an important area of study. Yearsley quotes Clodd on the significance of names:

> To the civilized man, his name is only a necessary label; to the savage it is an integral part of himself. [21]

In the fairy tale, the name indicates something about the person who bears it — a trait of character, a physical characteristic, or even a talent. Quite often Mme. d'Aulnoy explains in a parenthetical

---

[19] Madame d'Aulnoy, *Histoire d'Hypolite, Comte de Duglas* (Brusselles: George de Backer, 1704), p. 275.

[20] See p. 70.

[21] Yearsley, p. 165.

remark why the name is given to one of her characters. It may be for his physical appearance.

> On le nomma ainsi à cause de la couleur de son teint et de l'oranger où il demeurait. ("Le Nain jaune," I, p. 293)

> La reine sa mère voulut qu'on l'appelât Torticoli; soit qu'elle aimât ce nom ou qu'étant effectivement tout de travers, elle crût avoir rencontré ce qui lui convenait davantage. ("Le Rameau d'or," I, p. 149)

> Elle allait toujours dans une jatte, elle avait les jambes rompues. On l'appelait Trognon. ("Le Rameau d'or," I, p. 149)

> Sa beauté, sa douceur et son esprit, qui étaient incomparables, la firent nommer Gracieuse. ("Gracieuse et Percinet," I, p. 9)

> On l'appelait Truitonne, car son visage avait autant de taches de rousseur qu'une truite; ses cheveux noirs étaient si gras et si crasseux que l'on n'y pouvoit toucher et sa peau jaune distillait de l'huile. ("L'Oiseau bleu," I, p. 46)

> A quelque temps de là l'on apprit que le roi Charmant devait arriver. Jamais prince n'a porté plus loin sa galanterie et la magnificence; son esprit et sa personne n'avaient rien qui ne répondit à son nom. ("L'Oiseau bleu," I, p. 47)

> L'on avait nommé la jeune princesse Printanière, parce qu'elle avait un teint de lys et de roses, plus frais et plus fleuri que le printemps. ("La Princesse Printanière," I, p. 116)

The name may also indicate a character trait.

> Elle voulut lui donner un nom qui inspirât du respect et de la crainte. Après avoir longtemps cherché, elle l'appela Furibon. ("Le Prince Lutin," I, p. 79)

> A cause de sa bonne grâce et de son esprit, on le nommait Avenant. ("La Belle aux cheveux d'or," I, p. 32)

A feat or adventure of the character is often significant enough to bring him a name.

> C'est ainsi qu'on le nommait depuis qu'il avait gagné trois batailles. (Le Prince Guerrier in "La Biche au bois," II, p. 84)

> On me nomme Carpillon, dit-elle.—Le nom est singulier, reprit le roi; et à moins que quelque aventure n'y ait donné lieu, il est rare de s'appeler ainsi. ("La Princesse Carpillon," II, p. 32)

A circumstance of birth may lead to the naming of a child.

> Nous sommes bien aises de vous annoncer que vous aurez une belle princesse que vous nommerez Désirée; car l'on doit avouer qu'il y a longtemps que vous la désirez. ("La Biche au bois," II, p. 79)

It may even be the purpose or intent the character has in the eyes of the namer.

> Les ogres sont de terribles gens: quand une fois ils ont croqué de la chair fraîche (c'est ainsi qu'ils appellent les hommes), ils ne sauraient presque plus manger autre chose. ("L'Oranger et l'abeille," I, p. 179)

The name changes in "Finette Cendron," "Serpentin vert," and "Le Rameau d'or" are due to an inner change in the characters, or at least to an inner virtue displayed by the characters. The clever youngest in "Finette Cendron" is Fine-Oreille. It is she who overhears the parents' plan to abandon her two sisters and herself.

> Leurs majestés furent bien surprises de revoir les princesses; ils en parlèrent toute la nuit, et la cadette qui ne se nommait pas Fine-Oreille pour rien, entendait qu'ils faisaient un nouveau complot. (I, p. 242)

It is as if Finette takes a different name for each new motif that is introduced. As the clever youngest who overhears that the parents want to abandon them, she is Finette. When she and her sisters take over the ogres' castle and she finds the key to the chest of beautiful clothes in the hearth, she is Cendron.

> La maîtresse du logis vint à elle, et lui ayant fait une profonde révérence, elle la pria de lui dire comment elle s'appelait, afin de ne jamais oublier le nom d'une personne si

merveilleuse. Elle lui répondit civilement qu'on la nommait Cendron. (I, p. 249)

When she tries on the slipper and it fits proving that she will become the bride of Prince Chéri, she is called Princesse Chérie.

En même temps l'on crie: Vive la princesse Chérie, vive la princesse qui sera notre reine. (I, p. 253)

Hence, the three names indicate her three roles — clever youngest of abandoned children is Finette, tender of the hearth is Cendron, and beautiful princess is Chérie.

Two other heroines who change names are Trognon of "Le Rameau d'or" and Laideronnette of "Serpentin vert." Both have ugly or deformed bodies at the beginning and both are offered the choice of becoming beautiful or having a beautiful soul. Since they choose the latter, they receive the outward beauty as a symbol of their inner virtue. When the King Trasimène grants a wish to the deformed Trognon, she chooses a beautiful soul.

Rendez mon âme aussi belle que mon corps est laid et difforme. (I, p. 162)

Naturally, such a choice also merits a beautiful outward appearance:

"Ah, princesse, s'écria le roi Trasimène, vous me charmez par un choix si juste et si élevé; mais qui est capable de le faire est déjà accomplie: votre corps va donc devenir aussi beau que votre âme et votre esprit." Il touche la princesse avec le portrait de la fée; elle entend cric, croc dans tous ses os; ils s'allongent, ils se remboîtent; elle se lève, elle est grande, elle est belle, elle est droite, elle a le teint plus blanc que du lait, tous les traits réguliers, un air majestueux et modeste, une physionomie fine et agréable. "Quel prodige! s'écrie-t-elle. Est-ce moi? Est-ce une chose possible?—Oui, madame, reprit Trasimène, c'est vous; le sage choix que vous avez fait de la vertu vous attire l'heureux changement que vous éprouvez. Quel plaisir pour moi, après ce que je vous dois, d'avoir été destiné pour y contribuer! Mais quittez pour toujours le nom de Trognon; prenez celui de Brillante que vous méritez par vos lumières et par vos charmes." (I, p. 162)

What an amazing metamorphosis this is! A legless, deformed lass sprouts legs with a simple "cric, croc" that makes them grow right before our eyes.

Laideronnette, too, chooses to drink the water of discretion in order to beautify her soul. Automatically, it changes her physical appearance as well as her soul. The protective fairy congratulates her and adds,

> Puisque vous êtes si belle, je souhaite que vous quittiez le nom de Laideronnette qui ne vous convient plus, il faut vous appeler la reine Discrète. (I, p. 332)

A happy ending is soon in store for Discrète and her green serpent husband because of her discretion.

A similar transformation takes place in Torticoli, the hero destined to be Trognon's husband. He disenchants the fairy, Bénigne, who grants him a favor. His first interest is in her behalf. She insists that he ask for something for himself.

> "Madame, dit le prince, en se jetant à ses pieds, vous voyez mon affreuse figure, on me nomme Torticoli par dérision; rendez-moi moins ridicule.—Va, prince, lui dit la fée, en le touchant trois fois avec le rameau d'or, va, tu seras si accompli et si parfait, que jamais homme devant ni après toi, ne t'égalera; nomme toi *Sans-Pair,* tu porteras ce nom à juste titre." (I, p. 156)

With this last name change we complete the different types of transformations found in Mme. d'Aulnoy's *Contes des fées.* They are vivid depictions of all the various types of metamorphoses previously witnessed in Apuleius or Ovid.

It would be an oversight in any study of metamorphoses not to look into Ovid, that master of the art of transforming, to see what insights he might offer on our current analysis. Horace Gregory pointed out in his translation of *The Metamorphoses* that Ovid believed in the transformation of all things.

> Ovid's nature of things was the nature of transformations. He did his best to make Pythagorean theory support the large design of *The Metamorphoses.* He had rounded out his conception of a world he had promised to reveal in Book I. However shallow many of Ovid's convictions were,

he held to his belief that nothing in the world could be destroyed; all things become transformed — and not least, his own poetry into an immortality. [22]

Mme. d'Aulnoy's transformations seem more whimsical in that they are wrought by fairies rather than by gods. She believes in the mutability of all things, but not once and for all. Her transformations, rather, point up man's duality. They are evidence of good and evil in mankind and are brought about by beneficient and malevolent fairies, or, as we shall see in the following chapter, by love. There are a number of traits that the two authors do have in common. Both are baroque and both treat the same themes — metamorphoses and love. Ovid's treatment of women shows a knowledge of feminine psychology equal to Mme. d'Aulnoy's. She, like Ovid before her, uses asides to comment on emotional situations. Even the morals in both have an ironic ring. However, despite these commonalities, any influence from Ovid on Mme. d'Aulnoy probably came through La Fontaine.

There are also some similarities to Dante in the *contes*. The most obvious one is when the characters are doing penance and they meet humans who have been transformed into their animal counterparts so that the punishment suits the sin. In "Serpentin vert" the canary talks to Discrète as the shades spoke to Dante.

Il faut que vous sachiez, madame, que plusieurs fées s'étant mises à voyager, se chagrinèrent de voir des personnes tombées dans des défauts essentiels, elles crurent d'abord qu'il suffirait de les avertir de se corriger: mais leurs soins furent inutiles, et venant tout à coup à se chagriner, elles les mirent en pénitence; elles firent des perroquets, des pies et des poules de celles qui parlaient trop; des pigeons, des serins et des petits chiens, des amants et des maîtresses; des singes de ceux qui contrefaisaient leurs amis; des cochons de certaines gens qui aimaient trop la bonne chère; des lions des personnes còleres; enfin le nombre de ceux qu'elles mirent en pénitence fut si grand, que ce bois en est peuplé de sorte que l'on y trouve des gens de toutes qualités et de toutes humeurs. (I, pp. 332-33)

---

[22] Ovid: *The Metamorphoses,* A Complete New Version by Horace Gregory (New York: The Viking Press, 1958), pp. xxvi-xxvii.

The following passage even reminds us of Francesca and Paola. The young canary who speaks to tell his story was formerly the son of a Spanish nobleman.

> "Je te condamne, dit-elle, à devenir serin de Canarie pour trois ans, et ta maîtresse mouche-guêpe." Sur-le-champ, je sentis une métamorphose en moi la plus extraordinaire du monde; malgré mon affliction, je ne pus m'empêcher de voler dans le jardin de l'ambassadeur, pour savoir quel serait le sort de sa fille; mais j'y fus à peine, que je la vis venir comme une grosse mouche-guêpe, bourdonnant quatre fois plus haut qu'une autre. Je voltigeais autour d'elle avec l'empressement d'un amant que rien ne pouvait détacher; elle essaya plusieurs fois de me piquer. "Voulez-vous ma mort, belle guêpe, lui dis-je, il n'est pas nécessaire pour cela d'employer votre aiguillon, il suffit que vous m'ordonniez de mourir." (I, p. 333)

In the underworld of "La Grenouille bienfaisante" there is a similar situation.

> Tous les monstres dont ce lac est couvert, reprit Grenouillette, ont été dans le monde; les uns sur le trône, les autres dans la confidence de leurs souverains, il y a même des maîtresses de quelques rois, qui ont coûté bien du sang à l'état: ce sont elles que vous voyez métamorphosées en sangsues: le destin les envoie ici pour quelque temps, sans qu'aucun de ceux qui y viennent retourne meilleur et se corrige. (II, p. 57)

The very fact that the fairy tales deal with other worlds is a parallel to Dante. Tolkien is most explicit in stating the importance and necessity of this Secondary World in works of fantasy.

> What really happens is that the story-maker proves a successful "sub-creator." He makes a Secondary World which your mind can enter. Inside it, what he relates is "true": it accords with the laws of that world. You therefore believe it, while you are, as it were, inside. The moment disbelief arises, the spell is broken: the magic, or rather art, has failed. You are then out in the Primary World again, looking at the little abortive Secondary World from outside. [23]

---

[23] Tolkien, p. 37.

Mme. d'Aulnoy's Secondary Worlds are crystal palaces that appear and disappear mysteriously according to the whims of the fairies or pleasure islands with such lovely sounding names as "l'île de la Félicité" or "l'île déserte des écureuils." Often the Other World is entered via "une grande galérie" as in "Le Rameau d'or" or by a stairway as in "La Grenouille bienfaisante." There, the queen is led to an underground inferno comparable to any of Dante's *bolgie*.

> Quelle surprise et quelle douleur pour la reine, de se voir dans cet affreux séjour! l'on y descendait par dix mille marches, qui conduisaient jusqu'au centre de la terre; il n'y avait point d'autre lumière que celle de plusieurs grosses lampes qui réfléchissaient sur un lac de vif-argent. Il était couvert de monstres, dont les différentes figures auraient épouvanté une reine moins timide; les hiboux et les chouettes, quelques corbeaux et d'autres oiseaux de sinistre augure s'y faisaient entendre; l'on apercevait dans un lointain une montagne d'où coulaient des eaux presque dormantes; ce sont toutes les larmes que les amants malheureux ont jamais versées, dont les tristes amours ont fait des réservoirs. Les arbres étaient toujours dépouillés de feuilles et de fruits, la terre couverte de soucis, de ronces et d'orties. La nourriture convenait au climat d'un pays si maudit; quelques racines sèches, des marrons d'Inde et des pommes d'églantier, c'est tout ce qui s'offrait pour soulager la faim des infortunés qui tombaient entre les mains de la fée Lionne. (II, pp. 55-56)

The monsters and other horrible creatures recall some of the tormented described by Dante. In "Le Nain jaune" the King of the Gold Mines has to confront four sphinxes, six dragons and twenty-four nymphs before arriving at the steel castle where his princess is. The use of fabulous beasts is reminiscent of the allegorical procession in Paradise.

There are prophecies and dreams throughout the *contes* just as there were throughout *La Divina Commedia*. The best example is Merveilleuse's dream in "Le Mouton" which her father interprets as a threat to his own sovereignty and which causes him to send her to be killed. The prophecy of the fairies in "La Princesse Rosette" almost comes true.

Nous craignons, madame, que Rosette ne cause un grand malheur à ses frères; qu'ils ne meurent dans quelque affaire pour elle. (I, p. 133)

Finally, the fairy tale lends itself to the same four levels of interpretation as the *Commedia*. On the literal level the fairy tale portrays man's experiences in a Secondary World. Allegorically, man is torn between good and evil. Morally, good is rewarded and evil is punished and anagogically, it might be the depiction of essential processes within the soul.

The point here is not that Mme. d'Aulnoy was influenced by Dante, but that her work, too, has a depth and an interest that makes it universal. Heuscher, perhaps, expresses best the lasting value of the fairy tale.

> It might be more accurate to point out that the genuine fairy tale aims at maintaining, furthering and perfecting in the human being everything that is beyond the animal instincts. [24]

In this chapter on metamorphoses and grateful animals we have discussed all of Madame d'Aulnoy's *contes de fées* except "La Princesse Rosette." Yet, it has a place here, too, for it treats a young princess who wants to marry a peacock. She will have no other for her husband than the king (since she is a princess) of peacocks. Her brothers set out to look for him with grave doubts.

> Si le roi des paons est un paon lui-même, comment notre sœur prétend-elle l'épouser? Il faudrait être fou pour y consentir. Voyez la belle alliance qu'elle nous donnerait: des petits paonneaux pour neveux. (I, p. 137)

Although the peacock is neither a grateful animal helper nor a human under metamorphosis, it does offer an example of a "bête prenant le masque d'un homme" which brings us full circle from our initial premise concerning Madame d'Aulnoy's animals. It is appropriate that we conclude the animal treatment with this tale since it, more than any of the others, forebodes the eighteenth

---

[24] Julius E. Heuscher, *A Psychiatric Study of Fairy Tales, Their Origin, Meaning and Usefulness* (Springfield: Charles C. Thomas, 1963), p. 126.

century moral and philosophical hypotheses à la Espinasse.[25] It is possible that the animal fables of La Fontaine and the metamorphoses of Mme. d'Aulnoy served as the prelude to later discussions by the *philosophes* on the mixing of the species.

As we have witnessed, Mme. d'Aulnoy keeps in her *contes* a number of the traditional beliefs and themes. The name change in line with inner transformations, grateful animals and myriad metamorphoses recall the primitive beliefs that the name is an integral part of the person and that "the germs of folk-tale were also those of myth and like all the mental workings of uncivilized man, they show the predominance of imagination over reason."[26]

---

[25] See Diderot's *Entretien entre Diderot et d'Alembert, Le Rêve de d'Alembert, Suite de l'Entretien* (Paris: Garnier, 1965), where they discuss the "mélange des espèces" and "chèvre-pieds," pp. 181-86.

[26] Yearsley, p. 17.

CHAPTER V

LOVE AS A THEME

THE INFLUENCE of the Cupid and Psyche myth is evident in many
of Mme. d'Aulnoy's tales, especially those where the main interest
is love. It is mentioned specifically in several of the *contes* such
as "Gracieuse et Percinet," "La Princesse Félicité et le Prince
Adolphe," "Serpentin vert," "Le Prince Lutin," and suggested in
numerous others. La Fontaine, as pointed out earlier, exerted an
influence on Mme. d'Aulnoy metamorphoses, but it may be that
his influence extended to her treatment of love as well. In his
Amours de Psyché et de Cupidon, La Fontaine introduces many of
the love motifs that are dealt with throughout Mme. d'Aulnoy's
Contes des fées. There are separations, prohibitions, penances, invisible lovers, shepherdesses, oracles and always heroes or heroines
who are perfect in beauty and who are put to the test for their
love.

   The major love motifs from Cupid and Psyche are the heroine's
perfect beauty, the jealousy of a goddess or even a stepmother, a
supernatural lover (probably invisible), prohibitions, curiosity, pun-
ishments with tasks imposed, the lover-helper's return, a possible
visit to the underworld, the reunion of the lovers and the apotheosis of the heroine. The fairy tale that is patterned almost entirely
after the Cupid and Psyche myth is "Grecieuse et Percinet." Gracieuse is beautiful physically and morally.

> Sa beauté, sa douceur et son esprit, qui étaient incompara-
> bles, la firent nommer Gracieuse. (I, p. 9)

Gorgnon, her future stepmother, is eaten up with jealousy of Gracieuse's beauty.

> Ces sortes de monstres portent envie à toutes les belles
> personnes: elle haïssait mortellement Gracieuse, et se retira
> de la cour pour n'en entendre plus dire de bien. (I, p. 9)

Percinet is not a god, but he does have the ability to become
invisible.

> Le don de féerie que j'ai reçu en naissant m'a été d'un
> grand secours pour me procurer le plaisir de vous voir.
> (I, p. 13)

Gracieuse is punished by her stepmother for a mishap that was not
her fault. First, she is whipped, but Percinet turns the sticks to
feathers. When she awakes from her feigned malady, Percinet is
in her room.

> Elle lui dit qu'elle n'oublierait de sa vie les obligations
> qu'elle lui avait; qu'elle le conjurait de ne la pas aban-
> donner à la fureur de son ennemie, et de vouloir se retirer,
> parce qu'on lui avait toujours dit qu'il ne fallait pas de-
> meurer seule avec les garçons. Il répliqua qu'elle pouvait
> remarquer avec quel respect il en usait; qu'il était bien
> juste, puisqu'elle était sa maîtresse qu'il lui obéit en toutes
> choses, même au depens de sa propre satisfaction. (I, p. 16)

There are two special circumstances here that deserve closer attention, for they mark a divergence from the Cupid and Psyche legend
and point clearly to a special form of love known as *amour
courtois.* Gracieuse shows her appreciation to Percinet for saving her from
a beating, but immediately she remembers that a young lady should
never remain alone ("demeurer seule") with a young man. Therefore, she asks him to leave and he, ever obedient ("il lui obéit en
toutes choses") to his lady's wishes, acquiesces. This is in keeping
with courtly love as defined by M. de Rougemont in his classic
work on love in Western civilization.

> Love further implies a ritual — the ritual of *domnei* or
> *donnoi,* love's vassalage. It is by the beauty of his musical
> homage that a poet wins his *lády.* On his knee he swears
> eternal constancy to her, as knights swore fealty to their

suzerain. He receives from her a golden ring and a chaste kiss on his brow. Thereupon the "lovers" are bound by the rules of *cortezia*: secrecy, patience, and moderation — the last not being altogether synonymous with chastity, but meaning rather restraint. . . . And especially a man has to be the *servente* of a woman.[1]

This is the kind of love that prevails throughout the *contes de fées*. Most of Mme. d'Aulnoy's fairy tale heroes obey and serve their mistress just as Percinet does even at the expense of his own satisfaction. He enters a tourney to defend his lady's beauty against Grognon's. As a result, Gracieuse is led to the woods and left alone for the wild animals to devour. She cries out for Percinet, asking if he has abandoned her. Yet, when a crystal palace appears, she hesitates before it.

> Je suis seule, disait-elle; ce prince est jeune, aimable, amoureux; je lui dois la vie. Ah! c'en est trop! éloignons-nous de lui. Il vaut mieux mourir que de l'aimer. (I, p. 18)

Another facet of courtly love is the lady who continues to say "no." It is an unsatisfied love. M. de Rougemont establishes the premise that courtly love derives from the dualism caused by the Cathars and the Catholics in the twelfth century. For the former, marriage was condemned; for the latter, it was a sacrament. Thus, in order to reconcile the two conflicting elements in their lives, the troubadours evolved what has come to be known as *cortezia*. The *leys d'amor,* its system of rules, were set down early in the twelfth century.

> They were Moderation, Service, Prowess, Long Expectation, Chastity, Secrecy and Pity, and those virtues led to Joy, which was the sign and guarantee of Vray Amor or True Love.[2]

Our heroine is following the rules of courtly love when she avoids being alone with her lover. However, Percinet appears and chastises her for avoiding him when he holds such great respect for her.

---

[1] Denis de Rougemont, *Love in the Western World,* trans. by Montgomery Belgion (New York: Fawcett World Library, 1956), p. 79.

[2] Rougemont, p. 124.

Vous me fuyez, lui dit-il, ma princesse; vous me craignez quand je vous adore. Est-il possible que vous soyez si peu instruite de mon respect, que de me croire capable d'en manquer pour vous? Venez, venez sans alarme dans le palais de féerie, je n'y entrerai pas si vous me le défendez. (I, p. 18)

Percinet speaks to her again on the way to the palace but she is ever careful to obey the rules of *bienséance* or decency even when they are alone, or perhaps especially when they are alone.

"Depuis que vous y êtes, ma princesse, répliqua Percinet, il n'y a plus dans cette sombre solitude que des plaisirs et d'agréables amusements: les amours vous accompagnent, les fleurs naissent sous vos pas." Gracieuse n'osa répondre: elle ne voulait point s'embarquer dans ces sortes de conversations, et elle pria le prince de la mener auprès de la reine sa mère. (I, p. 18)

As Percinet shows her around the palace, she observes her own life story engraved on the walls. Percinet explains that everything that has to do with her interests him. After dinner there is a performance of an opera based on the loves of Cupid and Psyche. A young shepherd appears on the stage to sing a song which mentions Gracieuse by name and alludes to her refusal to love. Her reaction is one of embarrassment.

Elle rougit de s'être entendu nommer devant la reine et les princesses; elle dit à Percinet qu'elle avait quelque peine que tout le monde entrât dans leurs secrets. (I, p. 19)

Her desire for secrecy, too, is a part of courtly love since the *secretum meum* serves to protect the lady from the *losengiers* or gossips. Yet, in spite of Percinet's efforts to serve her and suffer for her love, she remains unhappy in the palace because she has not fulfilled her *devoir*.

Si j'étais la maîtresse de ma destinée, lui dit-elle, le parti que vous me proposez serait celui que j'accepterais; mais je suis comptable de mes actions au roi mon père; il vaut mieux souffrir que de manquer à mon devoir. (I, p. 20)

Consequently she returns to her father's palace and further abuse from her stepmother. Before she leaves Percinet's crystal palace and before it breaks into a thousand pieces, thus shattering her illusions, Percinet prophesies:

> Mon palais sera parmi les morts; vous n'y entrerez qu'après votre enterrement. (I, p. 21)

This implies that she must die for her love as did Tristan and Iseult or Romeo and Juliet. We must remember that during the time between Tristan and Mme. d'Aulnoy's tales there were many developments in the treatment of love. Aside from the Platonic and Ovidian influences throughout the ages, the most direct influence on the French fairy tales of the seventeenth century seems to have been the allegorical novels of the early part of that century and Honoré d'Urfé's *L'Astrée*. They brought about — in fact, they insisted upon — the happy ending. Therefore, Gracieuse returns to her father, is given further impossible tasks by Grognon, including the usual winding of threads, sorting of feathers and transporting of a box she is forbidden to open. These last two are reminiscent of those Psyche carried out. With Percinet's help, Gracieuse manages to accomplish all of them to Grognon's dismay. As a last resort, Grognon pushes Gracieuse into a well so that Percinet's prophecy is fulfilled by her being buried metaphorically, just as Celadon and Astrée were saved by a metaphorical death. Now she explains why she has continued to refuse Percinet:

> Que ma destinée est terrible! s'écria-t-elle, je suis enterrée toute vivante! ce genre de mort est plus affreux qu'aucun autre. Vous êtes vengé de mes retardements, Percinet, mais je craignais que vous ne fussiez de l'humeur légère des autres hommes, qui changent quand ils sont certains d'être aimés. (I, p. 28)

This reference is a perfect example of *amour courtois* of the seventeenth century. The lady is more preoccupied with her own *vertu* than with the worth of her lover. Fortunately, Percinet appears with his mother and sisters to say that it is time to leave her miserable state and make him happy. The usual magnificent wedding takes place with all of the fairies in attendance including the evil one who helped Grognon plan Gracieuse's tasks. Her appearance provides a rather unique end to this tale. She apologizes and then sets out to get her revenge on Grognon by wringing her neck.

We have examined carefully one of the tales which is apparently based on the Cupid and Psyche theme. It is interesting to note that M. Huet substantiates the position of this paper, for he concludes that something of the Cupid and Psyche myth reached the middle ages through Apuleius.[3] This assumption coupled with the numerous Cupid and Psyche motifs pointed out here suggest that even though Mme. d'Aulnoy's tales are literary, many of the motifs are drawn from tradition. Mme. d'Aulnoy's forte is in the blending of these older motifs with the newer ideas of her own age, thus appealing to man's instinctive yearning for primitive beliefs while keeping him in touch with his own times.

The next *conte* that follows some of the motifs from Cupid and Psyche is "Serpentin vert." While "Gracieuse et Percinet" is the first tale in Mme. d'Aulnoy's *Contes des fées,* "Serpentin vert" is the last in the same volume. All of the other tales to be discussed here as having similar motifs are from the first volume. Thus, the influence of the Cupid and Psyche myth may be felt throughout the first volume. In lieu of a beautiful heroine in "Serpentin vert," we have Laideronnette, the antithesis of Psyche or Gracieuse, for the evil fairy made her perfect in ugliness ("parfaite en laideur"). She is so unsightly that she asks her parents if she might not lead a solitary life in order to hide her ugliness. She ends by boarding a boat that hits a rock and being saved by a green serpent whom she had previously disdained because of its ugliness. She awakes in a lovely palace presided over, not by voices as in the Cupid and Psyche legend nor by nymphs as in La Fontaine's *Amours de Psyché et de Cupidon,* but by the most charming little creatures ever created by the imagination. The *pagodes,* as they are called, are unusual looking and possess rather bizarre qualities.

> Les plus grands avaient une coudée de haut, et les plus petits n'avaient pas plus de quatre doigts; les uns beaux, gracieux, agréables; les autres hideux et d'une laideur effrayante. Ils étaient de diamants, d'émeraudes, de rubis, de perles, de cristal, d'ambre, de corail, de porcelaine, d'or, d'argent, d'airain, de bronze, de fer, de bois, de terre; les uns sans bras, les autres sans pieds, les bouches à l'oreille,

---

[3] Urban T. Holmes, *History of Old French Literature* (New York, 1962), p. 172.

des yeux de travers, des nez écrasés; en un mot, il n'y a
pas plus de différence entre les créatures qui habitent le
monde qu'il y en avait entre ces pagodes. (I, p. 317)

Il y avait quelquefois des pagodes qui avaient le ventre si
enflé, et les joues si bouffies, que c'était une chose surpre-
nante. Quand elle leur demandait pourquoi ils étaient ainsi
ils lui disaient: "Comme il ne nous est pas permis de rire,
ni de parler dans le monde, et que nous y voyons faire
sans cesse des choses toutes risibles, et des sottises presque
intolérables, l'envie d'en railler est si forte, que nous en
enflons, et c'est proprement une hydropisie de rire dont
nous guérissons dès que nous sommes ici." La princesse
admirait le bon esprit de la gent pagodine; car effective-
ment l'on pourrait bien enfler de rire, s'il fallait rire de
toutes les impertinences que l'on voit. (I, p. 320)

In spite of the entertaining traits of the *pagodes,* it is not long
before Laideronnette becomes unhappy with her life there. A voice
speaks to her saying he is the sovereign of this kingdom and he
adores her. Laideronnette cannot believe that anyone who could
see her would love her. The invisible suitor assures her that he is
sincere.

Je ne vous ai point trouvée telle que vous vous représentez,
et soit votre personne, votre mérite ou vos disgrâces, je
vous le répète, je vous adore, mais mon amour respectueux
et craintif m'oblige à me cacher. (I, p. 321)

The hero here resembles Cupid in that he will not allow himself
to be seen, but he resembles Percinet and the *soupirants* of *L'Astrée*
in his respect for his lady. She seems transformed by his love, for
she is no longer ugly in his eyes. Like Cupid, he marries Laideronnette with the stipulation that she will not see him until his penance
is completed in two years. Otherwise, he will have to begin his
seven years anew and she will have to share his woes. Interestingly
enough, one of the *pagodes* presents her with a copy of the Psyche
legend.

Il y en eut un qui apporta l'histoire de Psyché, qu'un
auteur des plus à la mode venait de mettre en beau langage; elle y trouve beaucoup de choses qui avaient du rapport à son aventure. (I, p. 324)

Doubtless, this refers to La Fontaine's *Amours de Psyché et de Cupidon*. The similarities between it and her own story have just begun. She, like Psyche, longs to see her parents and the *pagodes* are sent to bring them to the palace. Although Laideronnette reads and rereads the story of Psyche so as to be on guard against any such happenings, she comes to the same end as Psyche, for her curiosity wins over her love or her good judgment and she violates his prohibition to look at him.

> Mais quels cris épouvantables ne fit-elle pas lorsque au lieu du tendre Amour, blond, blanc, jeune et tout aimable, elle vit l'affreux Serpentin Vert, aux longs crins hérissées? (I, p. 325)

So begin the many tasks that Laideronnette must perform in order to disenchant her husband from the spell of the evil fairy Magotine. She weaves fine nets, plucks four-leaf clovers, obtains the water of discretion and drinks some of it. Thereafter, her outward beauty equals her inner beauty so that her protective fairy renames her Discrète. Her last task takes her to Proserpine's world for the essence of long life. Through the efforts of her protective fairy and *Amour*, she disenchants her husband, who is transformed into a handsome prince.

> L'Amour ne voulut pas les abandonner; il les conduisit chez Magotine, et pour qu'elle ne le vit pas, il se cacha dans leur cœur. (I, p. 339)

This remarkable love also moves the wicked Magotine.

> Elle reçut très bien ces illustres infortunés et faisant un effort de générosité surnaturelle, elle leur rendit le royaume de Pagodie. (I, p. 339)

In the moral verse at the end of this tale, Mme. d'Aulnoy alludes to both Pandora and Psyche.

> Sur un secret qui doit nous rendre misérables
>   Pourquoi vouloir ouvrir les yeux?
> Le beau sexe a surtout cette audace cruelle.
> Sur elle on nous a peint et Pandore et Psyché,
>   Qui voulant percer un mystère

Que les dieux aux mortels voulaient tenir caché,
Deviennent les auteurs de leur propre misère.
(I, p. 339)

This reference to Eve, the first female mortal, recalls Wallace
Fowlie's conclusion on the duality of the Christian concept of
woman.

Henceforth, the life of each individual man, as well as the
drama of all humanity, unfolds between the actions of two
women, between Eve, instrument of corruption, and Mary,
instrument of redemption.[4]

"Serpentin vert" illustrates the pull between good and evil within
the heroine who condemns her lover to longer penance through her
curiosity, but who also saves him. This tale displays a number of
the Cupid and Psyche motifs: the invisible or supernatural hero, the
jealous evil fairy, prohibitions, curiosity, tasks, a visit to the underworld and if not an apotheosis of the heroine, at least a magnificent
transformation from Laideronnette to Discrète!

"Gracieuse et Percinet" and "Serpentin vert" are classified by
Paul Delarue as Type 425B — the search for a lost spouse.[5] Two
other tales are similarly classified, "Le Mouton" and "L'Oiseau
bleu." The tales previously discussed deal primarily with this type
while these last two have other principal themes, the prince as a
bird in "L'Oiseau bleu" and the dream in "Le Mouton," so that
the search for a spouse is only a secondary motif. At the end of
"L'Oiseau bleu" the heroine, Florine, goes in pursuit of her lost
bird lover. An old lady provides her with four eggs which aid her
in reaching King Charming. In "Le Mouton" the motif is even less
significant since the sheep encounters no obstacles in arriving at
the palace where the lady he loves is attending her sister's wedding.
However, when he cannot gain admittance, he dies of grief.

Quand il fut au palais du roi, il demanda Merveilleuse;
mais comme chacun savait déjà son aventure, et qu'on ne
voulait plus qu'elle retournât avec le mouton, on lui refusa

---

4 Wallace Fowlie, *Love in Literature, Studies in Symbolic Expression*
(Bloomington: Indiana University Press, 1965), p. 23.
5 Paul Delarue, *Le Conte populaire français,* II (Paris, 1957), pp. 77-81.

durement de la voir; il poussa des plaintes, et fit des regrets capables d'émouvoir tout autre que les suisses, qui
regardaient la porte du palais. Enfin, pénétré de douleur, il
se jeta par terre et y rendit la vie. (I, p. 235)

The two additional tales that are related to Cupid and Psyche
are "Le Prince Lutin" and "Le Prince Adolphe et la Princesse Félicité." Both have invisible heroes, both of whom love a fairy.
Lutin is the perfect courtly lover whose greatest pleasure is in
serving his lady. Since he remains invisible, the princess imagines
that he is ugly. Abricotine, her lady-in-waiting, reminds her of
Psyche's experience.

> Quel dommage, disait-elle, que ce Lutin soit difforme et
> affreux! car se peut-il des manières plus gracieuses et plus
> aimables que les siennes?—Et qui vous a dit, madame,
> repliqua Abricotine, qu'il soit tel que vous vous le figurez?
> Psyché ne croyait-elle pas que l'amour était un serpent?
> Votre aventure a quelquechose de semblable à la sienne,
> vous n'êtes pas moins belle. Si c'était Cupidon qui vous
> aimât, ne l'aimeriez-vous point?—Si Cupidon et l'inconnu
> sont la même chose, dit la princesse en rougissant, hélas!
> je veux bien aimer Cupidon! (I, p. 106)

Prince Adolphe receives the gift of invisibility from Zéphire, the
main attendant in Psyche's palace.

> Je vais vous enlever, Seigneur, lui dit-il, comme j'enlevai
> Psyché par l'ordre de l'Amour, lorsque je la portai dans ce
> beau palais qu'il lui avoit bâti.[6]

Adolphe enters the palace and spends three hundred years with his
mistress. Unfortunately, he is the typical seventeenth-century hero,
for he begins to worry about his *vertu* and his *gloire* and leaves
to perform some deed to make him worthy of his lady. Delarue
lists this tale as Type 470B — The Land where one never dies,
but, as we have seen here, a number of similarities to Cupid and
Psyche are evident.

The last tale that treats the search for a lost spouse is "La
Grenouille bienfaisante." A queen is captured by a lioness and

---

[6] Mme. d'Aulnoy, *Histoire d'Hypolite* (Brusselles: George de Backer,
1704), p. 271.

taken to an underworld. If it were not for a frog (bewitched fairy) who befriends her and takes a message to her husband, the poor queen and her daughter Moufette, who was born in the underworld, would never have been rescued. This is also an example of married love that is constant. When the king learns of the queen's death,

> il pensa mourir lui-même de douleur; cheveux arrachés, larmes répandues, cris pitoyables, sanglots, soupirs, et autres menus droits du veuvage, rien ne fut épargné en cette occasion.
> Après avoir passé plusieurs jours sans voir personne, et sans vouloir être vu, il retourna dans sa grande ville, traînant après lui un long deuil, qu'il portait mieux dans le cœur que dans ses habits. (II, p. 61)

When we recall the strained relationship between Mme. d'Aulnoy and her husband after she and her mother had him accused of lèse-majesté, we may think that she emphasizes the sincerity of the king's mourning because of the hollowness of her own. Although most of the tales end with the wedding of the hero and the heroine, this is one of the few tales that treat married love. It is not surprising that she chose to treat it so seldom when we recall her own marriage of convenience to a man at least twenty-five years her senior.

Renée Riese Hubert writes of Mme. d'Aulnoy's very different conception of love:

> Il s'agit chez elle d'un sentiment complexe qui se développe d'une façon particulière dans chaque histoire. [7]

Other critics refer to her sensibility, not only in her novels, but in her fairy tales as well. In a relevant article, Shirley Jones identified some of the characteristics of novels of sensibility as being a preoccupation with virtue, an emphasis on love as involuntary passion, the innocence of the protagonists who suffer and a penchant for moral refinement. [8] Many of the protagonists of the *Contes des*

---

[7] Renée Riese Hubert, "L'Amour et la Féerie chez Madame d'Aulnoy," *Romanische Forschungen*, LXXV (1963), 1.

[8] Shirley Jones, "Examples of Sensibility in the Late Seventeenth Century Feminine Novel in France," *Modern Language Review*, LXI (April, 1966), 208.

fées are virtuous and suffer an innocent love. Those tales involving pastoral elements are especially subject to these influences. In "Le Rameau d'or," both the hero and the heroine are transformed from ugly, distorted beings into beautiful human beings called Sans-Pair and Brillante. They find themselves as shepherd and shepherdess in a forest. They are drawn to each other immediately, but since she is ever aware of propriety, she flees him thinking he is of a different social status.

> Quoi! j'ai le malheur d'aimer, disait-elle, et d'aimer un malheureux berger! Quelle destinée est la mienne? J'ai préféré la vertu à la beauté: il semble que le ciel, pour me récompenser de ce choix, m'avait voulu rendre belle; mais que je m'estime malheureuse de l'être devenue! Sans ces inutiles attraits, le berger que je fuis ne serait point attaché à me plaire, et je n''aurais pas la honte de rougir des sentiments que j'ai pour lui. (I, p. 166)

Sans-Pair, too, is afflicted.

> Que mon sort est cruel, s'écriait-il! quoique je fusse affreux, je devais succéder à mon pére. Un grand royaume répare bien des défauts. Il me serait à présent inutile de me présenter à lui ni à ses sujets, il n'y en a aucuns qui puissent me reconnaître; et tout le bien que m'a fait la fée Bénigne, en m'ôtant mon nom et ma laideur, consiste à me rendre berger, et à me livrer aux charmes d'une bergère inexorable, qui ne peut me souffrir. Etoile barbare, disait-il en soupirant, deviens-moi plus propice, ou rends-moi ma difformité avec ma première indifférence! (I, p. 166)

Later, she explains to him in verse (usually reserved for those utterances that lovers cannot seem to make in prose) that she flees him because reason is her guide. After this statement, Sans-Pair swoons from grief.

> Ah! vertu sévère et trop farouche, pourquoi redoutez-vous un homme qui vous a chérie dès sa plus tendre enfance? Il n'est point capable de vous méconnaître, et sa passion est toute innocente. (I, p. 167)

Brillante vacillates between what her heart feels and what her head dictates.

Son cœur voulait qu'elle rentrât dans le bois où elle avait laissé Sans-Pair; mais sa vertu triompha de sa tendresse. Elle prit la généreuse résolution de ne le plus voir. (I, p. 168)

She even seeks an enchanter to cure her of her love for the shepherd. However, he is an evil enchanter and turns her into a grasshopper when she spurns his love. Sans-Pair, while searching for her everywhere, meets an evil fairy who changes him into a cricket. They meet as grasshopper and cricket and follow the advice of a voice that tells them to seek the golden bough. Only when they resume their natural forms and are informed by the good fairy Bénigne that they are of equal rank do they think their love possible. Their concerns with virtue, with reason over innocent passion, with their sufferings, all point to Mme. d'Aulnoy's sensibility.

Similar loves are described in "Le Pigeon et la colombe" and in "La Princesse Carpillon." In the former the princess becomes a shepherdess to avoid a giant who is enamored of her. On the first meeting between the prince and this shepherdess "leurs regards et leurs actions marquaient assez les sentiments qu'ils avaient déjà l'un pour l'autre" (II, p. 197). Yet, the prince, realizing the difference in their rank, avoids her. Soon he fears that she loves another and becomes so jealous that he plants a spy to observe her. At the same time, she is experiencing the pangs of unrequited love.

> Cette aimable personne s'était aperçue avec dépit, que le prince l'avait si fort négligée, qu'il ne l'aurait pas revue si le hasard ne l'eût conduit dans le lieu où elle chantait; elle se voulait un mal mortel des sentiments qu'elle avait pour lui; et s'il est possible d'aimer et de haïr en même temps, je puis dire qu'elle le haïssait parce qu'elle l'aimait trop. Combien de larmes répandait-elle en secret! (II, p. 203)

The prince falls dangerously ill because of his passion for this simple shepherdess. Only she is able to cure him with her herbs and her glances.

> On appela ses médecins, ils demeurèrent surpris de l'excellence d'un remède dont les effets étaient si prompts; mais quand ils virent la bergère qui l'avait appliqué, ils ne s'étonnerent plus de rien, et dirent en leur jargon, qu'un de ses regards était plus puissant que toute la pharmacie ensemble. (II, p. 208)

When the prince is well, the queen mother sends him away and sells the shepherdess, Constancia, to a slave ship. The prince returns and sets out to find his love. He encounters one last test of his love at a forge where Cupid jumps out to admonish him not to throw himself into the fire unless his love is pure.

> Jette-toi dans ce feu, répliqua l'enfant, et souviens-toi que si tu n'aimes pas uniquement et fidèlement, tu es perdu. (II, p. 224)

The fire transforms him into a pigeon so that he can fly to the tower where Constancia is and save her from the giant. With a magic ring that he brings her, she becomes a dove and they fly off together, happy to remain birds, free from the woes of the world.

> Oui, mon cher prince, j'y consens; choisissons un pays agréable, et passons sous cette métamorphose nos plus beaux jours; menons une vie innocente, sans ambition et sans désir, que ceux qu'un amour vertueux inspire. (II, p. 232)

The separations, suffering and other obstacles to their love, as well as the emphasis on virtuous love are marks of this tale's sensibility.

"La Princesse Carpillon" is another pastoral tale with traits of sensibility. Aside from the characteristics already mentioned in other *contes,* there is one new element of sensibility that merits mention here. The protagonists are fond of shedding tears and displaying their emotions.

> Que ne se disaient-ils pas de tendre et de passionné! tout ce que le cœur peut ressentir, et tout ce que l'esprit peut s'imaginer, ils se l'exprimaient dans des termes si touchants, qu'ils fondaient en pleurs; et peut-être encore que l'on ferait bien pleurer quelqu'un en les redisant. (II, p. 50)

This leads directly into the sensibility of the novels in the eighteenth century in that the hero and the heroine show less restraint and more freedom in declaring their love.

The more we try of classify Mme. d'Aulnoy's treatment of love, the more it becomes obvious that she presents a different facet of it in almost every tale. While we have just seen examples of innocent, virtuous love, we cannot make the generalization that all of her tales depict this kind of sentiment. On the contrary, several introduce real passion or unnatural love, and others suggest a kind of love bordering on the erotic.

"La Princesse Printanière" and "La Belle aux cheveux d'or" are apt expressions of Arthurian romance in that the hero is sent as messenger from his lord to the lady. In winning the lady for his lord, he falls in love with the lady and she with him. Thus, the hero's fealty is divided between his lord and his lady ("mi dons"). Princess Printanière suggests to Fanfarinet that they elope with some of her parents' jewels and he pledges his undying love.

> Je jure, dit-il, à votre altesse, une fidélité et une obéissance éternelles. Grande princesse, vous faites tout pour moi, que ne voudrais-je pas faire pour vous! (I, p. 122)

When Fanfarinet asks where she wants to go, her reply is swift and shows plainly that there is no debate between duty and love in her mind. "Hélas! dit-elle, je veux aller avec vous; je n'ai que cela dans l'esprit" (I, p. 122). No sooner are they on the island than he grows so hungry that he abandons all thought of love. A voice wakes her with a warning that her lover plans to eat her.

> Ouvrant vite les yeux, elle aperçut à la lueur de son escarboucle, que le méchant Fanfarinet avait le bras levé, prêt à lui percer le sein de son epée; car la voyant si grassette et si blanchette, et ayant bon appétit, il voulait la tuer pour la manger. (I, p. 129)

Printanière kills her lover and is later wedded to Merlin's son as planned, but she is careful not to mention her previous affair. The moral states clearly that "je veux que la raison soit toujours souveraine" (I, p. 132).

Avenant of "La Belle aux cheveux d'or" performs tasks in order to win the lady for his lord. Even though she offers him her love and her kingdom, he remains loyal to his master.

> Elle le trouvait bien aimable, et elle lui disait quelquefois: "Si vous aviez voulu, je vous aurais fait roi; nous ne serions point partis de mon royaume." (I, p. 41)

Even after her marriage she prefers Avenant.

Il l'épousa avec tant de réjouissances que l'on ne parlait
d'autre chose; mais la Belle aux cheveux d'or qui aimait
Avenant dans le fond de son cœur, n'était bien aise que
quand elle le voyait et elle le louait toujours. (I, p. 41)

The king, naturally, becomes jealous and has Avenant put in the
tower. Obligingly, the king mistakes some poison water for magic
water to make him handsome and dies as a result. As soon as she
hears of the king's death she goes to Avenant.

> Elle se souvint aussitôt des peines qu'il avait souffertes à
> cause d'elle, et de sa grande fidélité: elle sortit sans parler
> à personne, et fut droit à la tour, où elle ôta elle-même
> les fers des pieds et des mains d'Avenant, et lui mettant
> une couronne d'or sur la tête et le manteau royal sur les
> épaules, elle lui dit: "Venez, aimable Avenant, je vous fais
> roi, et vous prends pour mon époux." (I, pp. 42-43)

Other tales display qualities of what Renée Riese Hubert calls
Baroque love.

> Selon la tradition Baroque, le thème de l'amour se dégage
> à travers des méandres de déguisement, de tromperies, de
> métamorphoses, de méconnaissances, de substitutions. [9]

The heroine of "Belle-Belle ou le Chevalier Fortuné" dons a male
disguise so that she can fulfill her father's obligation in the king's
army. The king's sister falls in love with this Chevalier Fortuné.

> La reine déçue par son habit, pensait sérieusement au
> moyen de contracter avec lui un mariage secret; l'inégalité
> de leur naissance était l'unique chose qui lui faisait de la
> peine. (II, p. 162)

The king declares his love for Belle-Belle when it is revealed that
she is not a *chevalier*.

> L'on courut annoncer ces surprenantes nouvelles au roi,
> qui s'abandonnait à une profonde tristesse. Dans ce mo-
> ment la joie prit la place de la douleur; il courut dans la
> place, et fut charmé de voir la métamorphose de Fortuné.

---

[9] Hubert, p. 4.

Les derniers soupirs de la reine suspendirent un peu les transports de ce prince; mais comme il réfléchit sur sa malice, il ne put la regretter, et résolut d'épouser Belle-Belle. (II, p. 188)

There are instances of love tromperies in Mme. d'Aulnoy's "Le Dauphin" and in "L'Oiseau bleu." In the latter, the ugly sister receives King Charming's ring under false pretenses.

La nuit était si noire qu'il aurait été impossible au roi de s'apercevoir de la tromperie qu'on lui faisait, quand bien même il n'aurait pas été aussi prévenu qu'il l'était, de sorte qu'il s'approcha de la fenêtre avec des transports de joie inexprimables: il dit à Truitonne tout ce qu'il aurait dit à Florine pour la persuader de sa passion. (I, p. 51)

In the former, a grateful dolphin provides the ugly hero with the ability to transform himself into a canary to be near his love, Livorette. Not only does she allow the canary, Biby, to remain in her room at night, but she becomes pregnant.

Biby était dans la chambre de Livorette; il ne jugea pas, comme les autres, que le médicin de campagne était un ignorant; il lui était venu plusieurs fois dans l'esprit que la princesse était grosse; il alla au bord du rivage pour consulter son ami le poisson, qui ne parut pas d'un autre sentiment. (II, p. 333)

Livorette's father casts all three of them out to sea. The dolphin takes them to his own island and builds them a beautiful palace, but Livorette clings to her honor and her duty when Alidor asks her to wed him.

Ah! lui dit-elle, seigneur, mon dessein est fixe là-dessus, je n'y consentirai de ma vie, qu'avec la permission du roi mon père et de la reine ma mère ... Vous jugez mal de mes sentiments, lui dit-elle, je vous estime, je vous aime, et je vous ai pardonné tous les maux que vous m'avez attirés par une métamorphose que vous ne deviez point tenter; car étant fils de roi, ne pouviez-vous pas croire que mon père se ferait un plaisir de vous voir dans son alliance? (II, pp. 343-44)

Her parents repent of their deed and set out to find their daughter. By a strange occurrence, they are shipwrecked and brought to the

Dolphin Island. After a nice visit with the charming couple whom they do not recognize as their daughter and Alidor, the king and queen plan to leave. Alidor and Livorette trick the king and queen by planting jewels on them and accusing them of taking them. As they try to explain their innocence, Livorette falls on her knees.

> Sire, dit-elle, je suis l'infortunée Livorette que vous fîtes mettre dans un tonneau avec Alidor et mon fils, vous m'accusiez d'un crime auquel je n'ai jamais consenti; ce malheur m'est arrivé sans que j'en aie eu plus de connaissance que vos majestés. (II, p. 350)

Just a harmless little trick to prove her innocence! These *tromperies,* as Renée Hubert calls them, add humor and charm to the tales.

In "Babiole" she and her cousin play a sort of trick on her mother so she will consent to their marriage. He pretends to be a necromancer.

> Madame, lui dit'il, j'étudie dès ma plus tendre jeunesse l'art de nécromancien; ... mais essuyez vos pleurs, madame, cette Babiole que vous avez vue si laide, est à présent la plus belle princesse de l'univers; vous l'aurez bientôt auprès de vous, si vous voulez pardonner à la reine votre sœur, la cruelle guerre qu'elle vous a faite, et conclure la paix par le mariage de votre infante avec le prince votre neveu. (I, pp. 287-88)

As for the metamorphoses and their role in the amorous developments, they range from animals loving humans (Babiole and Marcassin) to humans loving animals (Rosette and the Chatte blanche). Babiole, a monkey, loves her cousin and wins him only after she receives her human form. Marcassin, on the other hand, insists on being wedded to three sisters. In fact, it is the act of the three marriages that brings about his disenchantment. The third fairy, whose curse caused all of Marcissin's troubles, reveals her reason at the end.

> Il faut un peu diversifier la matière, le printemps serait moins agréable s'il n'était précédé par l'hiver; afin que le prince que vous souhaitez charmant, le paraisse davantage, je le doue d'être Marcassin, jusqu'à ce qu'il ait épousé trois femmes, et que la troisième trouve sa peau de sanglier. (II, p. 315)

This could be Mme. d'Aulnoy's theme song, that is diversifying the matter, for she manages to provide a different twist to each metamorphosis, to each form of love and to every protagonist. No two tales are alike, no two heroes are similar, nor are the plots reducible to any sort of easily recognizable plan. This is the reason that we chose to discuss her tales by themes.

The young man who is led to the white cat's fairy palace is impressed with his hostess from the outset.

> Madame la Chatte, dit le prince, vous êtes bien généreuse de me recevoir avec tant d'accueil, mais vous ne me paraissez pas une bestiole ordinaire; le don que vous avez de la parole, et le superbe château que vous possédez, en sont des preuves assez évidentes. (II, p. 115)

He later becomes so enamoured of this "bestiole pas ordinaire" that he makes a strange wish.

> Il regrettait quelquefois de n'être pas chat, pour passer sa vie dans cette bonne compagnie. "Hélas! disait-il à Chatte Blanche, que j'aurai de douleur de vous quitter; je vous aime si chèrement! ou devenez fille, ou rendez-moi chat." (II, p. 118)

However, his wish is not granted. At the end he must cut off her head and tail, those animal characteristics, and throw them into the fire and out comes the most beautiful princess in the world.

> Il coupa la tête et la queue de sa bonne amie la Chatte: en même temps il vit la plus charmante métamorphose qui se puisse imaginer. Le corps de Chatte Blanche devint grand et se changea tout d'un coup en fille; c'est ce que ne saurait être décrit, il n'y a eu que celle-là d'aussi accomplie. (II, p. 127)

The cat then tells the story of how she became a cat and of how she could only be disenchanted by a man who resembled her former husband. Her first marriage to a young king is similar to Printanière's passion for Fanfarinet. He insists that she come down from her fairy tower or let him come up. She finally makes a ladder from nets and sends him word.

Sans attendre que je descendisse, il monta avec empresse-
ment, et se jeta dans ma chambre comme je préparais tout
pour ma fuite.

Sa vue me donna tant de joie, que j'en oubliai le péril
où nous étions. Il renouvela tous ses serments, et me con-
jura de ne point différer de le recevoir pour mon époux:
nous prîmes Perroquet et Toutou pour témoins de notre
mariage. Jamais noces ne se sont faites, entre des personnes
si élevées, avec moins d'éclat et de bruit, et jamais cœurs
n'ont été plus contents que les nôtres. (II, p. 141)

So it is that we find two forms of love in the same tale. The white
cat's first love is full of passion and quickly fulfilled, while her
second is a virtuous love that must be tested, but is lasting.

The young prince in the preceding tale loves a white cat who
becomes, through his efforts, a beautiful princess. In "La Princesse
Rosette" a young princess, who is locked in a tower because of a
prophecy that she would cause her brothers to come to misfortune
or death, is set free only to fall in love with a peacock!

Elle leur montra le paon, et leur demanda ce que c'était
que cela? Ils lui dirent que c'était un oiseau dont on man-
geait quelquefois. "Quoi, dit'elle, l'on ose tuer un si bel
oiseau et le manger? Je vous déclare que je ne me marierai
jamais qu'au roi des paons, et, quand j'en serai la reine,
j'empêcherai bien que l'on n'en mange." (I, p. 136)

The brothers set out to find the king, wondering what type of
nephews they will have from such a union. [10] The king agrees to
wed Rosette if she is as lovely as her portrait. However, a new
development of the Baroque makes its appearance here in the form
of a substitute bride. Delarue lists this tale and "La Biche au bois"
as Type 403 — the substitute fiancée. [11] Usually a nurse decides to
replace the princess with her own ugly daughter as surrogate bride
of the king. Such is the case with Rosette, since the nurse throws
her off the ship and presents her own daughter in her place. The
king will have no part of the scheme.

Comment! dit-il, ces deux marauds que je tiens dans mes
prisons ont bien de la hardiesse de s'être moqués de moi

---

[10] See *supra,* p. 101.
[11] Delarue, II, pp. 52-53.

et de m'avoir proposé d'épouser une magote comme cela;
je les ferai mourir. (I, p. 142)

In "La Biche au bois" a fairy curse demands that Désirée become a doe if she sees daylight before reaching age fifteen. Her
lady-in-waiting, Longue-Epine, deliberately cuts a hole in the closed
carriage so that Désirée cannot proceed to marry Prince Guerrier.
No sooner is Désirée transformed than she runs off into the forest.
Longue-Epine (Long-Thorn) decks herself in finery and aspires to
marry the prince, but when he sees her:

> O dieux! que devint-il après avoir considéré cette fille,
> dont la taille extraordinaire faisait peur! Elle était si grande
> que les habits de la princesse lui couvraient à peine les
> genoux; sa maigreur affreuse, son nez, plus crochu que
> celui d'un perroquet, brillait d'un rouge luisant; il n'a
> jamais été de dents plus noires et plus mal rangées. Enfin
> elle était aussi laide que Désirée était belle. (II, p. 95)

The substitute bride is a theme as old as the story of *La Reine
Pédauque* which R. Dévigne lists with "Les Grands thèmes légen-
daires." [12] It is the story of Berthe, Charlemagne's mother, and her
faithful servant, Margiste. The latter substitutes her own daughter
as bride for Pépin le Bref. Only later is the real bride discovered in
the woods and all is put right. It is strange that this legend of
La Reine Pédauque (Queen Goosefoot) is often confused with *la
mère l'oye*. It is a perfect example of how fact and fiction often
fuse in tradition. Stith Thompson, in discussing the substitute bride
type, connects it with *The Little Goose Girl* who is substituted in
the marriage bed since the king has a magic stone that indicates the
bride's chastity. [13] Could there be some link between the surrogate
bride and the universal tension which Fowlie spoke of between
Eve and Mary, between evil and good? Could not the Mother
Goose tale assure us of the good?

This may seem far removed from the theme of love in Mme.
d'Aulnoy's tales, but, in reality, it proves that true love will win

---

[12] R. Dévigne, *Le Légendaire des provinces françaises à travers notre folklore* (Paris: Horizons de France, 1950), pp. 219-40.
[13] Stith Thompson, *The Folktale* (New York: The Dryden Press, 1946),
pp. 119-20.

out in fairy tales if not always in real life. It provides another facet of Mme. d'Aulnoy's already varied offering. With these last few tales of disguises, tricks, metamorphoses, and substitutions, we conclude the tales that can be considered primarily baroque.

The final tales to be considered here have a love interest, but it is secondary to the main motifs of the plot or it is there simply as an adjunct to a happy ending. In "La Bonne petite souris" the fairy mouse puts Joliette on the throne of the evil king and announces to the people that they will look for a handsome prince to wed the charming Joliette.

> Au réveil de la jeune princesse, la fée lui présenta le plus beau prince qui eût encore vu le jour. Elle l'était allé quérir dans le char volant jusqu'au bout du monde; il était tout aussi aimable que Joliette. Dès qu'elle le vit, elle l'aima. (I, p. 218)

The young heroine, "Fortunée," is faced with a similar situation. She disenchants her cousin whom the queen intends for her to marry, but Fortunée is reticent.

> Madame, répliqua-t-elle en rougissant, vous me comblez de grâces, je connais que vous êtes ma tante; que par votre savoir, les gardes envoyés pour me tuer, ont été métamorphosés en choux, et ma nourrice en poule; qu'en me proposant l'alliance du prince Œillet, c'est le plus grand honneur où je puisse prétendre. Mais, vous dirai-je mon incertitude? Je ne connais point son cœur, et je commence à sentir pour la première fois de ma vie que je ne pourrais être contente s'il ne m'aimait pas. (I, p. 262)

Prince Oeillet (Carnation) preens, sighs, and writes verses to Fortunée in order to win her as his bride. She does consent, finally, but only because she has not seen any other who equals him.

> Il la conjurait de prendre une résolution en sa faveur: enfin elle y consentit; elle n''avait rien vu d'aimable, et tout ce qui était aimable, l'était moins que ce jeune prince. (I, p. 264)

Finette's Prince Chéri seems to fall in love with her red velvet slipper rather than with her.

> Le lendemain le prince Chéri, fils aîné du roi, allant à la chasse, trouve la mule de Finette; il la fait ramasser, la regarde, en admire la petitesse, et la gentillesse, la tourne, retourne, la baise, la chérit et l'emporte avec lui. (I, p. 250)

Even when she discovers that the slipper fits, Finette is not emotional.

> "Vive la princesse Chérie, vive la princesse qui sera notre reine!" Le prince se leva de son lit, il vint lui baiser les mains, elle le trouva beau et plein d'esprit: il lui fit mille amitiés. (I, p. 253)

Finette is more concerned with practical matters such as seeing her parents' kingdom restored and her sisters forgiven than in basking in her own love. It may be that Mme. d'Aulnoy has already exhausted two motifs in this story, that of the abandoned children and the ogres' being deceived, and rather than dwell on the love theme, she is suggesting a logical conclusion. Certainly, Finette's strong feminine role throughout would lead her to consider others ahead of herself. This is not to suggest that she did not live happily ever after with her prince, but there are those few rare human beings who relish giving more than receiving. Finette's is a love that cannot be happy at the expense of others. Hers is the opposite of La Rochefoucauld's *amour propre*.

Another strong female character is Aimée of "L'Oranger et l'abeille." She saves her cousin, Aimé, from the ogres and takes the initiative in their magic flight. After their first metamorphosis, there is a passage that describes Aimé's love for his cousin and his hope that he will soon make her his wife.

> Ce qu'on ne croira peut-être pas sans peine, c'est qu'en attendant cet heureux jour, il vivait avec elle dans les bois, dans la solitude, et maître de lui proposer tout ce qu'il aurait voulu, d'une manière si respectueuse et si sage, qu'il ne s'est jamais trouvé tant de passion et tant de vertu ensemble. (I, p. 196)

There is a certain irony here that hints at Mme. d'Aulnoy's making fun of her own protagonists to the amusement of all. It is often said that the fantastic in the fairy tale is enjoyed by the child while the humor is relished by the adult. Mme. d'Aulnoy's humor and irony will be discussed in the next chapter.

The next couple is "Belle-Etoile et le Prince Chéri." The main motif concerns an abandoned wife who supposedly gave birth to dogs. Actually, her own children are put out to sea, found by a privateer and reared by him and his wife. There are three boys and one girl, and a very special feeling develops between Belle-Etoile and Chéri.

> Mais à quatorze ans Belle-Etoile commença de se reprocher de l'injustice qu'elle croyait à ses frères, de ne pas les aimer également. Elle s'imagina que les soins et les caresses de Chéri en étaient la cause. Elle lui défendit de chercher davantage les moyens de se faire aimer. (II, p. 246)

These two young people, like Francesca and Paolo, discover their true sentiments while reading a work that lays bare their own feelings.

> C'était l'histoire de deux jeunes amants, dont la passion avait commencé se croyant frère et sœur, ensuite ils avaient été reconnus par leurs proches, et après des peines infinies ils s'étaient épousés. (II, pp. 246-47)

Further in their text, the two protagonists are mentioned by name so that we learn that Mme. d'Aulnoy is referring to her own *Histoire d'Hypolite, Comte de Duglas* where we learn that a young boy and girl love each other while growing up thinking they are brother and sister.

> Ah, ma sœur! s'écria-t-il en la regardant tristement, et laissant tomber son livre, ah, ma sœur, qu'Hippolyte fut heureux de n'être pas le frère de Julie! —Nous n'aurons pas une semblable satisfaction, répondit-elle: hélas, nous est-elle moins due! (II, p. 247)

Hence, Mme. d'Aulnoy not only mentions her own previous fairy tales in her *Contes des fées,* but equates parallel motifs from other works to her *contes.* Love, then, is a theme of her novels as well as of her tales. Yet, in the novels it is all bound up with political schemes and courtly intrigues while in the fairy tale the obstacles to love are more from inner conflicts than from external forces.

Naturally, Belle-Etoile and Chéri learn they are not brother and sister and are subsequently promised to each other.

"Le Nain jaune," the last tale to be dealt with from the point of view of its love interest, is unique. It does not fit any of the other classifications in its treatment of love. In fact, we are not even convinced there is a real love in this story. Toute-Belle, the heroine, is so haughty and disdainful of all her suitors that it is hard to imagine her ever loving any other as much as herself. Her mother reminds her that those who seek her hand are worthy of her, but Toute-Belle remains unmoved.

> J'en serais fâchée si vous aimiez quelque chose au-dessous de vous; mais voyez ceux qui vous demandent, et sachez qu'il n'y en a point ailleurs qui les valent.
> Cela était vrai; mais la princesse prévenue de son mérite, croyait valoir encore mieux; et peu à peu, par un entêtement de rester fille, elle commença de chagriner si fort sa mère, qu'elle se repentit, mais trop tard, d'avoir eu tant de complaisance pour elle. (I, p. 292)

The worried mother goes to consult a desert fairy, is confronted by lions and saved by the yellow dwarf when she promises him her beautiful daughter. Toute-Belle goes to visit the desert fairy and, like her mother, is saved only after promising to wed the yellow dwarf. In spite of this she agrees shortly thereafter to marry the king of gold mines, but not out of love.

> Toute-Belle avait bien rabattu de sa fierté depuis son aventure avec le Nain jaune; elle ne comprenait pas de meilleur moyen pour se tirer d'affaire que de se marier à quelque grand roi, contre lequel ce petit magot ne serait pas en état de disputer une conquête si glorieuse. (I, p. 296)

When the desert fairy and the yellow dwarf come to claim her on her wedding day, the woes begin for Toute-Belle and her king. Jealousy at seeing the king with the desert fairy seems to awaken Toute-Belle's love.

> Quoi, s'écria-t-elle, ne suis-je donc pas assez malheureuse dans cet inaccessible château, où l'affreux Nain jaune m'a transportée? Faut-il que pour comble de disgrâce le démon de la jalousie vienne me persécuter? (I, p. 302)

At the end, the king saves her with a magic sword, but she receives him coldly since she still believes he has been untrue to her.

> Il l'aborde en tremblant; il veut se jeter à ses pieds; mais elle s'éloigne de lui avec autant de vitesse et d'indignation que s'il avait été le Nain jaune. (I, p. 309)

Meanwhile the yellow dwarf seizes the magic sword and threatens to kill the king if she does not agree to marry him. Neither can consent to that so it is in death that the lovers are united.

> Ces deux corps si parfaits devinrent deux beaux arbres, conservant toujours un amour fidèle l'un pour l'autre, ils se caressent de leurs branches entrelacées, et immortalisent leurs feux par leur tendre union. (I, p. 310)

This last love we would term self-interest since Toute-Belle is brought to it as a last resort. It is the opposite of Finette's love, yet it completes the cycle of love motifs in Mme. d'Aulnoy's tales with the emphasis on faithful love. After having observed her develop a variety of love situations throughout the *contes,* we can appropriately conclude our study with this tale that transforms a purely selfish love into an enduring faithful love, for "la petite baguette produit des effets encore plus extraordinaires" (I, p. 112).

CHAPTER VI

STYLE AND HUMOR

THE THEMES OF LOVE and metamorphosis, coupled with an insight
into the manners of seventeenth-century France as revealed in
Mme. d'Aulnoy's *Contes des fées,* are enhanced by her imaginative
style, her unusual vocabulary and her natural flow of language.
Edmond Pilon, in his *Muses et bourgeoises de jadis,* compares
Mme. d'Aulnoy with other women fairy tale writers of her era
and concludes that her contes "l'emportaient encore en charme et
en malice." [1] It is this ambiguity that intrigues the reader and
makes him plead for more.

A part of this charm and malice stems from her delightful,
enigmatic fairies. In later publications of her tales, the title becomes
*Les Contes des fées ou les enchantemens des bonnes et mauvaises
fées.* Their very names distinguish their malefic or benefic nature.
Tourmentine, Fanferluche, Feintise, Magotine, Ragotte and Carabosse are obviously to be feared while Gentille, Bénigne, Protectrice, Tulipe and Souveraine are just as obviously to be trusted.
Throughout the tales Mme. d'Aulnoy unmasks their equivocal
natures.

> J'ai de l'inquiétude de cette fée de belle humeur, car la
> plupart sont malicieuses, et ce n'est pas toujours bon signe
> quand elles rient. (II, p. 286)

This fairy causes the queen to give birth to a young boar. Later
the three fairies explain themselves.

---

[1] Edmond Pilon, *Muses et bourgeoises de jadis* (Paris: Editions Excelsior,
1933), p. 16.

Nous sommes trois sœurs, répliqua la fée; il y en a deux bonnes, l'autre gâte presque toujours le bien que nous faisons. (II, p. 299)

The queen in "La Princesse Carpillon" wonders what her family has done to deserve the fairy's protection.

J'ai toujours entendu dire, répliqua la reine, qu'il est de bonnes et de mauvaises fées, qu'elles prennent des familles en amitié ou en aversion selon leur génie. (II, p. 47)

Alidor in "Le Dauphin" simply sits on Grognette's rock, and she takes immediate dislike to him.

Il sentit que la roche s'agitait fortement, ensuite elle s'ouvrit pour laisser sortir une vieille petite naine déhanchée, qui s'appuyait sur une béquille: c'était la fée Grognette, qui n'était pas meilleure que Grognon. "Vraiment, dit-elle, seigneur Alidor, je te trouve bien familier de venir t'asseoir sur ma roche, je ne sais ce qui m'empêche te jeter au fond de la mer, pour t'apprendre que si les fées ne peuvent rendre un mortel plus heureux que toi, elles peuvent au moins le rendre malheureux dès qu'elles le veulent." (II, p. 330)

The fairy in "La Princesse Printanière" waits years to avenge the king for a childhood prank he played on her.

Hélas! ma mie, nous sommes perdus, dit le roi, c'est ici la fée Carabosse. La méchante me haïssait dès le temps que j'étais petit garçon, pour une espièglerie que je lui fis avec du soufre dans son potage. (I, p. 114)

The fairy who helps Gracieuse's stepmother with the tasks she imposes on Gracieuse later repents and goes back to strangle the stepmother. This is no more than poetic justice since the stepmother had tried to strangle her earlier.

Lorsque cette marâtre la vit revenir, elle se jeta sur la fée, qu'elle avait retenue; elle l'égratigna, et l'aurait étranglée, si une fée était étranglable. (I, p. 27)

Another example of poetic justice is seen at the end of "L'Oiseau bleu" when the deceiving sister is changed into the animal for whom she had been named.

> Dès qu'elle voulut ouvrir la bouche pour lui dire des injures, l'enchanteur et la fée parurent, qui la métamorphosèrent en truie, afin qu'il lui restât au moins une partie de son nom et de son naturel grondeur. (I, p. 77)

Mme. d'Aulnoy's fairies are not always all-powerful. Often they must elicit the help of an enchanter in order to carry out their magic ("L'Oiseau bleu"). There are also *demi-fées* whose efficacy is only half as influential as that of a full-fledged fairy. The fairies captivate us with the ingenuity of their magic, with their curses and their blessings, and especially with their penchant for performing all good or all evil deeds. We know the nature of their acts, but we are kept in suspense as to how they will bring it about.

Just as enchanting as the fairies is the animal-like vocabulary Mme. d'Aulnoy employs. It reveals an understanding of animals and a feeling for them that makes them real and winsome to the reader. To begin with, there is a whole new lexicon of verbs used to disenchant each species. Laideronnette will not be happy until her green serpent is "déserpentiné." The other fairies beg Carabosse to "déguignonner" Princesse Printanière. When Prince Marcassin is most depressed about his fate, a lady approaches him and assures him that he will soon be "démarcassiné." Some of these newly formed verbs are reflexive as if to imply that the personage can disenchant himself. These are used in cases where the characters are changing back and forth. Prince Lutin, for example, is endowed by a fairy whom he has helped: "Soyez lutin lutinant" (I, p. 84). He can become an invisible sprite or remain himself when it suits him. "Lutin, se délutinant, parut tout d'un coup à la porte de la salle" (I, p. 88). Désirée's curse makes her a doe ("biche") during the day, yet she resumes her own form at night. "L'heure de se débichonner étant arrivée, la belle reprit sa forme ordinaire" (II, p. 101). The hero of "Le Rameau d'or" has been given the clue to his own disenchantment by his protective fairy. "Il faut, dit-il, chercher le Rameau d'or, peut-être que je me dégrillonnerai" (I, p. 175).

Not only does Mme. d'Aulnoy create new verbs to discuss her animal characters, she also forms adjectives to describe those characteristics peculiar to each creature. Prince Marcassin's father wants to have the little monster drowned, but his mother protects him and tries to make him presentable at court. "Enfin, on lui ôtait, autant qu'il était possible, les manières marcassines" (II, p. 288). Further in the tale he begins courting a young lady, and we learn that he hasn't lost all of his boarish manners, for his gifts to the lady are not ordinary ones. "Il lui donnait toutes les truffes que son instinct marcassinique lui faisait trouver dans la forêt" (II, p. 291). How typically French for a young boar to provide his lady with the one delicacy that he alone can offer! There are many such passages of ironic humor throughout Mme. d'Aulnoy's *contes* that enliven her tales in a way that surpasses Perrault.

In "La Chatte blanche" there is a hunt. Quite naturally, their hunt is for birds. The master of the hunt is a monkey who brings the white cat an eagle's nest so that she can "disposer à sa volonté des petites altesses aiglonnes" (II, p. 117). The young hero is amazed at this strange pageantry. "Il lui semblât que tant de cha-tonnerie tenait un peu du sabbat ou du sorcier" (II, p. 117). However, our young hero has just begun to witness the strange happenings at this fairy court. When he returns on his third quest, Madame Minette orders a naval battle between her cats and the neighboring rats. The rats seem to be winning until her admiral makes a decisive move.

> Minagrobis, amiral de la flotte chatonnique, réduisit la gent ratonienne dans le dernier désespoir. Il mangea à belles dents le général de leur flotte. (II, p. 126)

The adjectives "chatonnique" and "ratonienne" add to the satiric effect of the whole war. This tale is so filled with feline terms that the reader experience the same feeling as the hero. "C'est peut-être le premier mortel qui se soit si bien diverti avec des chats, sans avoir d'autre compagnie" (II, p. 121). From his entrance past the history of famous cats to the music of the cat orchestra which begins to "miauler sur différents tons," and the white cat's greeting "Fils de roi, sois le bienvenu, ma miaularde majesté te voit avec plaisir" (II, p. 115) to her final request that he cut off her "cha-tonique figure," the whole atmosphere is filled with "cat-ness." It is Mme. d'Aulnoy's special animal vocabulary and her attention to details about these animals that set her tales apart from those of other fairy tale writers of the period. Her tales are a mixture of fable and fairy tale, combining the best features of both. They are didactic as when the hero of "La Chatte blanche" comes in out of a rainy night, "Il était mouillé comme je l'ai dit, et l'on avait peur qu'il ne s'enrhumât" (II, p. 114) and pleasing in that magic hands appear to undress him and warm before the fire, "les mains qui lui semblaient fort belles, blanches, petites, grassettes et bien proportionnées le déshabillèrent" (II, p. 114).

In other tales Mme. d'Aulnoy uses her animal vocabulary but to a lesser extent than in "La Chatte blanche." When the queen of "La Grenouille bienfaisante" arrives in the underworld, her first act is to save the frog from the crow. "La grenouilla tomba, resta quelque temps étourdie, et reprenant ensuite ses esprits grenouilliques" (II, p. 57), she speaks. The queen is amazed when the frog speaks to her. Mme. d'Aulnoy's interest in languages, and especially the desire to communicate with other creatures, is evident in many of the tales. When the monkey king, Magot, sends his ambassador to ask for Babiole's hand in marriage, he sends along a parakeet as interpreter and even a magpie as *sous-interprète*! Not only does the parakeet interpret, he writes poetry too. He addresses a rather lengthy poem to Babiole in behalf of his king. The ambassador delivers Magot's gifts to Babiole in person.

L'ambassadeur lui fit entendre en grommelant, qui est la langue dont on se sert en Magotie que son monarque était plus touché de ses charmes qu'il l'eût été de sa vie d'aucune guenon. (I, p. 273)

Babiole, although encompassed in a monkey's body, keeps her human heart. Therefore, she confesses her love to the prince, who makes fun of her and assures her she should marry Magot and adds "et en faveur de la bonne amitié entre nous, envoie-moi le premier Magotin de ta façon." Magot's kingdom, then, is "Magotie"; his people are "Magotins"; and they communicate "en grommelant."

The pigeon of "Le Pigeon et la colombe" regrets that he has not been given the power of speech as "L'Oiseau bleu" was. He tries to commit suicide by throwing himself from a high cliff, forgetting "quel secours peuvent être des plumes." He next decides to pluck out his feathers in order to try again. At this point two young girls find him and plan to put him in a pie for the fairy, Souveraine. When the fairy caresses him, his reaction and gestures are appealing.

Il lui faisait la révérence à la pigeonne en tirant un peu le pied; il la becquetait d'un air caressant: bien qu'il fût pigeon novice, il en savait déjà plus que les vieux pères et les vieux ramiers. (II, p. 227)

When the fairy tells him his love is being held in a tower by a giant and that her only help can come from his own willingness to fly to her with a magic ring that will enable her to become a dove and escape, he is impatient to be on his way.

Le pigeonneau était dans la dernière impatience de partir, il ne savait comme le faire comprendre; il tirailla la manchette et le tablier en falbala de la fée, il s'approcha ensuite des fenêtres, ou il donna quelques coups de bec contre les vitres. Tout cela voulait dire en langage pigeonique: "Je vous supplie, madame, de m'envoyer avec votre bague enchantée pour soulager notre belle princesse." (II, p. 229)

Mme. d'Aulnoy's description of his efforts to communicate is poignant. Who can remain unmoved before the poor bird's sad plight and his noble efforts to communicate "en langage pigeonique?" Later he is granted his speech again so that he can declare his love to his lady.

Another feature of Mme. d'Aulnoy's style is the use of personification. In "Belle-Etoile et le Prince Chéri" there is a singing apple ("la pomme qui chante"), a green bird of truth ("le petit oiseau vert qui dit tout") and water that dances ("l'eau qui danse"). In "L'Oranger et l'abeille" there is even a bean ("fève") that talks in order to answer the ogre's questions while Aimée escapes with her cousin. The strangest of the talking objects, however, appear in "Fortunée." It is as though Fortunée's kindnesses disenchant all the objects around her. The chicken talks and we learn she was the laborer's garrulous wife who was changed into a chicken because it was her nature to "caqueter." When Fortunée's brother replaces her carnation ("Oeillet") with a cabbage, she throws it out the window. To her amazement, the cabbage utters a complaint. "Ha! je suis mort. Elle ne comprit rien à ces plaintes, car ordinairement les choux ne parlent pas" (I, p. 258). Finally, the carnation speaks in order to declare his love for her. It is too much for poor Fortunée.

La princesse, tremblante et surprise d'avoir entendu parler un chou, une poule, un œillet et d'avoir vu une armée de rats, devint pâle et s'evanouit. (I, p. 261)

The *merveilleux* of this tale lacks the charm and humor of many of the other tales, most probably because it is not convincingly real. Mme. d'Aulnoy's animal vocabulary is missing, and with it, much of the allure of the tale. The magic seems artificial and contrived if compared with "Le Prince Mascassin," "L'Oiseau bleu," or even with "Belle-Etoile et le Prince Chéri," which also has talking objects in lieu of animals.

Some of Mme. d'Aulnoy's human characters have difficulty with their language too. Aimée of "L'Oranger et l'abeille" speaks the language of her foster parents, the ogres. "Elle ne savait ni lire, ni écrire, ni aucunes langues; elle parlait le jargon d'ogrelie" (I, p. 182). When she falls in love with her cousin, Aimé, who is shipwrecked on her island, they communicate through kinesics, ". . . leurs yeux et quelques gestes servaient d'interprètes à leurs pensées" (I, p. 184). In order to save Aimé from being eaten by the ogre, Aimée removes the crown from one of the little ogre's heads and places it on her cousin's. This is the same situation as in Perrault's "Le Petit Poucet." If we compare the passage by Perrault with Mme. d'Aulnoy's, we can note that Perrault simply states that the ogres wear a crown at night while Mme. d'Aulnoy explains the custom and the ogres' attitude toward the custon.

On les avait fait coucher de bonne heure et elles étaient toutes sept dans un grand lit, ayant chacune une Couronne d'or sur la tête.[2]

Or, c'est la coutume en ogrichonnerie, que tous les soirs, l'ogre, l'ogresse et les ogrichons, mettent sur leur tête une belle couronne d'or, avec laquelle ils dorment: voilà leur seule magnificence, mais ils aimeraient mieux être pendus et étranglés que d'y avoir manqué. (I, p. 190)

The addition of "la coutume en ogrichonnerie" and the enumerating of "l'ogre, l'ogresse et les ogrichons" contribute to the mocking

---

[2] G. Rouger, ed., *Contes de Perrault* (Paris: Editions Garnier, 1967), p. 193.

quality of the passage. The explanation of the ogres' strong feeling about their custom enhances the burlesque tone. Mme. d'Aulnoy even names her ogres Ravagio and Tourmentine while Perrault's remain impersonalized. After saving Aimé from Ravagio, Aimée steals Tourmentine's magic wand. Her first wish is that she speak the same language as the one she loves. Since she is new at this language, she explains her ineptness. "Mes expressions sont plus simples, répliqua la princesse, mais elles ne seront pas moins sincères" (I, p. 193).

All of these references to language indicate Mme. d'Aulnoy's overwhelming interest in language and words. She even based an entire local legend on one word in her *Relation du voyage d'Espagne*.[3] Mme. d'Aulnoy coins new words that suit her personages and add to their personalities at the same time. Marcassin would be just another ordinary boar without his "instincts marcassiniques" and the white cat would be only half as appealing without her "chatonique figure."

The manner in which her metamorphosed animals show emotions is ingenious. We have already referred to the pigeon's homage to the fairy by pecking her with a caressing manner ("becqueter d'un air caressant"). The fairy serpent in "Le Prince Lutin" is equally engaging when she flaunts all her charms before the young man who saved her life. "Dès qu'elle l'apercevait, elle venait au-devant de lui, rampant et faisant toutes les petites mines et les airs gracieux dont une couleuvre est capable" (I, p. 81). When Aimé and Aimée are changed into an orange tree and a bee, they are visited by Princess Linda who enjoys the fragrance of the orange blossoms. The bee stings Linda out of jealousy and the orange tree reprimands the bee.

> Elle pleura en cet endroit, autant qu'une Abeille est capable de pleurer; quelques fleurs de l'amoureux Oranger en furent mouillées, et son déplaisir d'avoir chagriné sa princesse alla si loin que toutes ses feuilles jaunirent, plusieurs branches séchèrent, et il en pensa mourir. (I, p. 201)

---

[3] Princess Mira was so named because everyone who saw her exclaimed "Look" (Mira). She was indifferent to all men until she saw Nios who was indifferent to her. She died of grief and her sighs still come from the castle. Foulché-Delbosc, pp. 187-88.

Thus a jealous bee cries and the leaves of a chagrined orange tree turn yellow and dry up when they have a lovers' quarrel. Mme. d'Aulnoy's personification of her animals and plants is singular in that it is truly personal. Not every tree will respond emotionally by drying up its leaves nor will every serpent crawl up to her guardian and flirt with him. All the animals and plants react individually and according to their nature. This is Mme. d'Aulnoy's own interpretation of Cartesianism. Serpentin Vert emotes quite differently from the fairy serpent of "Le Prince Lutin." He falls in love with Laideronnette, but she scorns him. "Serpentin Vert fit un long sifflement (c'est la manière dont les serpents soupiraient), et sans répliquer, il s'enfonca dans l'onde" (I, p. 315). None but a lady writer who understands and loves animals would think of a serpent's hiss as a sigh. Even her dolphin ("Le Dauphin") endeavors to empathize with his friend to the best of his ability. "Le Dauphin en eut pitié, il pleura un peu quoique les dauphins ne pleurent guère" (II, p. 334).

Mme. d'Aulnoy's humor is heightened by her own tongue-in-cheek remarks about some of the unusual happenings in her tales. For example, Prince Lutin profits from his invisibility to be near the princess he loves, yet he is not satisfied because "il est rare qu'un invisible se fasse aimer" (I, p. 103). Prince Adolphe, another invisible character, makes his way into Princess Felicité's garden, but finds no way of entering her palace. Finally, a basket is lowered from a window for the gardener to fill with flowers and Adolphe jumps in, hoping that his invisibility will also make him weightless. [4] When Torticoli's father seeks to arrange a marriage between his deformed son and Trognon, a legless cripple, her father is delighted, "car tout le monde n'est pas d'humeur de se charger d'un cul-de-jatte" (I, p. 150).

Another instance of such a comment is in "Belle-Belle ou le Chevalier Fortunée." Grugeon, one of the seven endowed ones, has just completed the task imposed by the emperor of eating all the bread baked in his city that day. As a result, no one has bread for supper that evening. "Il fallut que ce jour-là, depuis l'empereur jusqu'au chat, tout dînât sans pain" (II, p. 179). This attention to minor details intensifies the *vraisemblance* by adding a realistic

---

[4] See *supra*, p. 91.

touch. It reinforces the magic and makes it seem desirable, if not probable.

Many of Mme. d'Aulnoy's descriptions are filled with a similar mocking tone. When Fanfarinet comes to ask for Princess Printanière's hand for his lord, he is so dazzled by her beauty that he behaves like someone who is drunk.

> Fanfarinet avait beaucoup d'esprit, mais quand il vit la belle Printanière avec tant de grâces et de majesté, il demeura si ravi, qu'au lieu de parler, il ne faisait plus que bégayer; l'on aurait dit qu'il était ivre, quoique certainement il n'eût pris qu'une tasse de chocolat. (I, p. 120)

The comparison between a man who is struck speechless before a beautiful lady and a blubbering drunk may be apt, but the added explanation that he had had only one cup of chocolate is unexpected and, for that reason, it delights the reader all the more with its mockery. The description of the fairy frog's arrival at the king's palace with the message from his queen in the underworld is a perfect vignette of the manner in which women behave in court.

> Elle était un peu coquette de son métier, cela l'avait obligée de mettre du rouge et des mouches; l'on dit même qu'elle était fardée, comme sont la plupart des dames de ce pays-là; mais la chose approfondie, l'on a trouvé que c'étaient ses ennemis qu'en parlaient ainsi. (II, p. 62)

This passage is reminiscent of Perrault's irony in "Griselidis." Although he is dealing with a virtuous wife, he describes all the conniving women at court. Mme. d'Aulnoy's experience in courtly circles permits us this insight into petty comments and jealousies among the women at court. This is the reason many critics refer to her depiction of courtly society in her tales. Her personages exude the mentality and the language of the lords and ladies in the salons and at court.

There are also examples of exaggeration in Mme. d'Aulnoy's *contes*. We have referred to the fact that her characters are always perfect in beauty or sometimes perfect in ugliness (Laideronnette). In describing Finette Cendron, Mme. d'Aulnoy writes that "Finette était trente fois plus belle que la belle Hélène" (I, p. 252). Prince Marcassin recounts how he looked at himself in a stream and found his appearance so horrible that he cried. Then he adds, "Sans hyperbole, j'en versai assez [de pleurs] pour grossir le cours du ruisseau" (II, p. 315). When Belle-Belle and her seven endowed ones arrive at the Emperor Matapa's city, they are amazed at its size.

> Elle était plus grande que Paris, Constantinople et Rome ensemble; et si peuplée, que les caves, les greniers et les toits étaient habités. (II, p. 178)

At other times Mme. d'Aulnoy uses the technique of rhetorical questions. Perhaps the best example is when Laideronnette learns that she must go to the underworld to get the essence of long life for the evil fairy who has enchanted her beloved Serpentin Vert. She overcomes her surprise sufficiently to ask, "Par où va-t-on aux enfers?" (I, p. 336). The innocence with which it is uttered only adds to the irony. Another example is Carpillon's musing over the injustice of the way fate endowed the two men in her life.

> Pourquoi, disait-elle, bizarre fortune, donnes-tu tant de grâces, de bonne mine, et d'agrément à un jeune berger, qui n'est destiné qu'à garder son troupeau, et tant de malice, de laideur, et de difformité à un grand prince destiné à gouverner un royaume? (II, pp. 34-35)

These questions serve almost the same purpose as the asides to the reader which we mentioned earlier. [5] They both act as vents to the author's own mockery of the situation. They both add to the reader's pleasure, for they tend to give the reader the feeling that he, too, is a part of the burlesque. Such a case is when Babiole eats a nut given to her by King Magot and from the shell come architects, sculptors, masons and painters, who go to work immediately to build her a city five times the size of Rome. It was all done in three quarters of an hour. The aside states, "Voilà bien des prodiges sortis d'une petite noisette" (I, p. 281). The reader agrees, for he is thinking the same thoughts himself. Nevertheless, it delights us all the more to have the author emphasize the improbability of her own magic.

Another area of the magic in which Mme. d'Aulnoy excels is the naming of names. We alluded to some of the names earlier

---

[5] See *supra*, pp. 48-49.

when discussing the attributes of the heroes and heroines. [6] The names are certainly part of the charm and the humor of Mme. d'Aulnoy's *contes*. This is the reason we have not attempted to translate them in this work. The names are an integral part of the characters and they make them real, at least for the duration of the tale. Such an addition as calling the corsair's wife Corsine in "Belle-Etoile et le Prince Chéri" makes the wife authentic by establishing her firmly as part of a couple. The same is true of the ogres in "L'Oranger et l'abeille." They are not simply classified as ogres, they are given a name commensurate with their nature. He is Ravagio (Ravager) and his partner is Tourmentine (Tormentor). King Magot who sends ambassadors to ask for Babiole in marriage, is aptly named, for his name's literal meaning applies to his grotesque appearance and its figurative interpretation to the hidden treasures he gives Babiole which enable her to disenchant herself later. Emperor Matapa, the king's enemy in "Belle-Belle ou le Chevalier Fortuné," probably gets his name for killing the peace, which is truly an understatement if we consider his atrocities. The seven endowed ones in the same tale are identified by their talents. Hence, Forte-échine is strong; Léger is swift; le bon Tireur has exceptional vision; Fine-Oreille hears all; l'Impétueux has lungs strong enough to blow windmills; Trinquet is a great drinker and Grugeon is a heavy eater. There is never any question about a character's nature, for it is inherent in his name. Good and evil are easily distinguishable in the fairy tale.

Other qualities of Mme. d'Aulnoy's talent which enhance the appeal of these fantasies are her use of imitative harmonies and repetition. One example of the former is the "cric croc" that accompanies Trognon's metamorphosis in "Le Rameau d'or." She was a legless cripple, and with the simple "cric croc" she sprouted legs and became a lovely lady. The "tic toc" that Grognon makes knocking on the barrels filled with diamonds, pearls and other treasures in her *cave* recalls the techniques and sounds made by the traditional storytellers.

There are repetitions, usually to the customary tertiary rhythm of the fairy tale. For instance, in "La Belle aux cheveux d'or" each of the three animals Avenant helps repeats the same phrase, "Je

6 See *supra*, pp. 92-96.

vous revaudrai." Such a repetition satisfies in its simplicity and in its announcement of what is to come. We know that something will happen so that they will be able to repay the young hero's kindness. The same sort of repetition occurs in "Belle-Belle ou le Chevalier Fortuné" when each of the three sisters starts out disguised as a male. The first two sisters will not stop to help an old shepherdess whose sheep is in the ditch. To each the old lady calls out "Adieu, belle déguisée." They realize they have been discovered and return home. Only Belle-Belle helps the fairy shepherdess and receives her blessing.

Finally, Mme. d'Aulnoy uses a balanced structure of comparison that intensifies the good and evil duality of the fairy tale. In "La Chatte blanche" the king banishes the queen for having promised their daughter to the fairies in exchange for some fruit. The king soon relents and brings the queen back to court. "Il envoya quérir la reine avec autant de tendresse et de pompe qu'il avait fait mettre prisonnière avec colère et emportement" (II, p. 133). Whether the structure is labeled comparison or contrast, it serves both purposes. The structure uses comparison in the manner in which he sends her away and brings her back and uses contrast in the opposing intentions. The same structure is found in "Le Dauphin" and in "Serpentin vert." In the former story the contrast occurs in the previous trials of the prince and princess as opposed to the bliss of their married life.

> La vie du prince et de la princesse fut aussi longue et aussi heureuse qu'elle avait été triste et traversée dans les commencements. (II, p. 330)

The latter story is similar in that the tale concludes by alluding to their former misfortunes and their future happiness.

> Il y retournèrent sur-le-champ, et vécurent avec autant de bonne fortune qu'ils avaient éprouvé jusqu'alors de disgrâces et d'ennuis. (I, p. 339)

Such a structure as this contributes to the happy ending, for it enables us to observe how great their past tribulations were and it leaves us to anticipate how blissful their future will be. This is part of the solace of the happy ending in fairy tales, and Mme. d'Aulnoy magnifies it by the contrast.

In conclusion, Mme. d'Aulnoy's style makes her tales vivid and colorful. The magic of her enigmatic fairies is equaled only by the author's own mocking comments about their magic. Her animal vocabulary is comparable to La Fontaine's in its compassion for the creatures. The ironic humor of many passages surpasses Perrault's in its directness. Her tales may be comprised of mixed motifs from folklore, but her ingenuity blends each motif selected into one harmonious tale. She has also combined artistry with taste to produce twenty-five charming and entertaining *contes de fées*.

CONCLUSION

THE EVOLUTION of the fairy tale from a puerile pastime enjoyed in the salons of seventeenth-century France to a genre deemed worthy of serious scholarly attention all over the world in the twentieth century marks an intellectual development of almost three hundred years. That the *merveilleux* of the fairy tale exerted an influence on the philosophical *conteurs* of the eighteenth century is evidenced by the number of motifs and themes from Mme. d'Aulnoy's *contes de fées* that appear later in the fictional works of Voltaire and Diderot. In the nineteenth century it was the duality of good and evil, reality and illusion in the fairy tales of earlier writers such as Charles Perrault and Mme. d'Aulnoy that inspired a Charles Nodier or a George Sand to undertake to write their own fairy stories. With the flowering of the folklore movement and the analyses of fairy tales by Freud and Jung in the latter part of the nineteenth century, the fairy tale came into its own.

If no other phase of Mme. d'Aulnoy's *contes* were studied than the portrayal of contemporary manners, it would be revealing. Her accounts of the entertainments, the dances, the dress as well as the values and moral attitudes of her epoch are sweetness and light, for she makes the reader feel a part of the age of Louis XIV.

The main themes presented in Mme. d'Aulnoy's *contes de fées* are love and metamorphosis. The tales depict amorous love, maternal and filial love, friendship and such virtues as gratitude and clemency. Each of the twenty-five tales exemplifies some form of love. Each tale also represents some kind of transformation, ranging from a simple disguise to invisibility or a temporary change into another type creature or plant. The two themes unite to carry the message of love that transforms. The simplicity of the fairy tale makes it obvious that the outer transformation corresponds to the inner virtue.

Mme. d'Aulnoy's universal themes are developed in a style suitable to the subject. Her language of love is that of the courtly lover and her animal transformations are treated with a light irony that enhances the charm and appeal of the metamorphoses. The *contes* show a delicate balance between reason and magic, between classic and baroque that produces a believable kind of realism.

A CHRONOLOGICAL RESUME OF THE LIFE OF MARIE-CATHERINE LEJUMEL DE BARNEVILLE, BARONNE D'AULNOY [1]

1651 (?)—Although no birth or baptismal certificate has been located, this date is deduced from other documents as the year Marie-Catherine Lejumel de Barneville was born at the small Norman manor Barneville in the canton of Honfleur.

March 8, 1666—Marriage of Marie-Catherine and François de la Motte, Baron d'Aulnoy. She was fifteen and he was in his forties.

January 26, 1667—Birth of first child, Marie-Angélique, [2] who died young.

November 23, 1667—Birth of second child, Dominique-César, who died in infancy.

October 30, 1668—Birth of third child, Marie-Anne, who will become Mme. de Heère.

September 24, 1669 [3]—Baron d'Aulnoy was arrested for the crime of lèse-majesté due to the conniving of Mme. de Gudannes, his mother-in-law, and Mme. d'Aulnoy.

November 14, 1669—Birth of fourth child, Juliette-Henriette, who was to live in Spain and marry the Marquis de Bargento.

---

[1] Unless otherwise stated, the dates and facts listed here are found in Auguste Jal's *Dictionnaire critique de Biographie et d'Histoire,* 2nd ed., Paris: Henry Plon, 1872, pp. 1306-07.

[2] Since there are differing accounts of the number and names of Mme. d'Aulnoy's children, *Autour des Contes de feés, Recueil d'études de Jeanne Roche-Mazon,* Paris: Didier, 1968, p. 8, has been followed here as being the most comprehensive and the best documented.

[3] Mme d'Aulnoy, *Relation du Voyage d'Espagne* Avec une introduction et notes par R. Foulché-Delbosc, Paris: Librairie Klincksieck, 1926, p. 11, note 1.

November 1669 [4]—Lamorzière and Courboyer, fellow conspirators in the plot against the Baron d'Aulnoy, were executed.

January 13, 1670—M. d'Aulnoy released from Bastille.

October 14, 1676—Birth of fifth child, Thérèse Aymée, who was to become Mme. de Préaux d'Antigny. A sixth child, Françoise-Angélique-Maxime, lived in Spain and died in 1727 at age fifty. Her birth is derived from that as 1677.

1670-1690—Mme. d'Aulnoy was possibly in a convent during some of this period. She also traveled a great deal, possibly to England and to Spain. These are the mysterious twenty years according to J. Roche-Mazon (p. 149).

1679-1681—Mme. d'Aulnoy's trip to Spain is reputed to have taken place during these years if it took place at all.

1690 [5]—Publication of *L'Histoire d'Hypolite, Comte de Duglas* (containing first fairy tale) and *Mémoires de la cour d'Espagne.*

1691—Publication of *Relation du Voyage d'Espagne* and of *Les Sentimens d'une âme pénitente.*

1692—Publication of *Le Retour d'une âme à Dieu,* of *L'Histoire de Jean de Bourbon, Prince de Carency* and of *Les Nouvelles Espagnoles.*

1693—Publication of *Nouvelles ou Mémoires historiques.*

1694—Publication of *Mémoires de la Cour d'Angleterre.*

1697—Publication of *Les Contes des Fées.*

1698—Publication of *Les Contes nouveaux ou les Fées à la mode.* Elected to Académie des Picovrati in Padova. Mme. d'Aulnoy was Clio, muse of history.

1699—Mme. d'Aulnoy was almost involved in the assassination of M. Ticquet, "un conseiller au Parlement." She was a friend of Mme. Ticquet.

August 21, 1700—Death of Baron d'Aulnoy. His last act was to disinherit his wife, an act for which he was criticized by the general public.

1703—Publication of *Le Comte de Warwick.*

January 14, 1705—Death of Mme. d'Aulnoy at age fifty-four or fifty-five in her house in Paris, rue St.-Benoît.

---

4 Mme. d'Aulnoy, *Relation du Voyage d'Espagne,* p. 13.

5 For the dates of Mme. d'Aulnoy's literary works, see Foulché-Delbosc, pp. 110-20.

THE TWENTY-FIVE FAIRY TALES
AS THEY FIRST APPEARED[1]

Contes des Fées

Tome I.—(1) Gracieuse et Percinet.—(2) La Belle aux Cheveux d'or.—(3) L'Oiseau bleu.—(4) Le Prince Lutin.
Tome II.—(5) La Princesse Printanière.—(6) La Princesse Rosette.—(7) Le Rameau d'or.—(8) L'Oranger et L'Abeille.—(9) La bonne petite Souris.
Tome III.—(A) Don Gabriel Ponce de Leon, nouvelle.—(10) Le Mouton.—(11) Finette Cendron.—(12) Fortunée.
Tome IV.—(13) Babiolle.—(B) Don Fernand de Tolede, nouvelle.—(14) Le Nain.—(B) Suite de Fernand de Tolede, nouvelle.—(15) Serpentin vert.

Contes Nouveaux ou Les Fees a la Mode

Tome I.—(16) La Princesse Carpillon.—(17) La Grenouille bienfaisante.—(18) La Biche au Bois.
Tome II.—(C) Le Nouveaux Gentilhomme Bourgeois, nouvelle.—(19) La Chatte Blanche.—(C) Suite du Nouveau Gentilhomme Bourgeois, nouvelle.—(20) Belle-Belle, ou le Chevalier Fortuné.

---

[1] See Foulché-Delbosc's "Madame d'Aulnoy et l'Espagne" in Madame d'Aulnoy's *Relation du Voyage d'Espagne* (Paris, 1926), pp. 122-23. The twenty-fifth tale does not appear in the *Contes des fées,* but in Madame d'Aulnoy's first novel in which she may have been experimenting with the genre that was currently popular in the salons.

SUITES DES CONTES NOUVEAUX OU DES FEES A LA MODE

Tome III.—(C) Suite du Gentilhomme Bourgeois, nouvelle.—(21) Le Pigeon et la Colombe.—(C) Suite du Gentilhomme Bourgeois, nouvelle.—(22) La Princesse Belle-Etoile et le Prince Chéri.
Tome IV.—(C) Suite du Gentilhomme Bourgeois, nouvelle.—(23) Le Prince Marcassin.—(C) Suite du Gentilhomme Bourgeois, nouvelle.—(24) Le Dauphin.—(C) Suite du Gentilhomme Bourgeois, nouvelle.
(25) Le Prince Adolphe et la Princesse Félicité appeared in *Histoire d'Hypolite, Comte de Duglas* in 1690.

1. *Gracieuse et Percinet*:

A king and queen have only one daughter whom they name Gracieuse because she is sweet and pretty. Unfortunately, the queen falls ill and dies, leaving the king in a state of depression. Finally, his doctors order him to seek other diversions to take his mind off of his loss. One day, while hunting, he stops at a castle to rest. It is the castle of the duchess Grognon, an ugly old lady who is jealous of Gracieuse's beauty. She is, however, very rich. That very day the king agrees to wed her and to give her full jurisdiction over his daughter and, in turn, Grognon will give him barrels of money. Gracieuse goes into the forest to cry and Percinet, the green page, comforts her and reveals that he is a prince with magic gifts who loves her and will help her. When Grognon arrives and sees Gracieuse with a beautiful horse and page, she takes them both. The horse throws her and she blames Gracieuse, whom she punishes by having her whipped. Percinet saves her with his magic by making the sticks become feathers. In order to please Grognon, the king has her portrait made and holds a tourney with six knights defending Grognon's beauty. However, Percinet arrives, proclaiming his lady to be more beautiful, and overcomes all the knights. Again Grognon wants her revenge; so she has Gracieuse left in a deep forest for the animals to devour. Percinet arrives when she calls for him and takes her to a crystal palace. Through Percinet's magic she can see what is happening at court. She sees how her father grieves for her death, for Grognon has buried a log saying it is Gracieuse. She returns to court in spite of Percinet's telling her that she will never enter his palace again until after her burial.

Even though the king digs up the log, he still allows Grognon to convince him that it is not his daughter. Grognon puts Gracieuse through all kinds of trials with the aid of a fairy whom she sends for. The first task is to wind thread, the second to separate feathers of different birds and the third is to take a box to her castle without opening it. Naturally, Gracieuse would have been unable to perform these tasks without her loving Percinet. Finally, Grognon pushes Gracieuse into a well (buried!) and she enters a beautiful garden and finds herself before the fairy castle again. Percinet's mother tells Gracieuse that it is time to withdraw herself from the deplorable state in which she has lived with Grognon and to make Percinet happy by marrying him. A magnificent wedding takes place and all the fairies attend, including the one who helped Grognon with her tasks for Gracieuse. When she recognizes Gracieuse, she tries to make amends by hastening back to Grognon and chocking her to death.

Moral: Envy causes human ills. Love with constancy.

2.   *La Belle aux cheveux d'or*:

A king and queen have a beautiful daughter. A young king from a neighboring kingdom sends his ambassador with gifts to ask for her in marriage. The daughter refuses and sends back the gifts. There is a handsome young man in the kingdom who is highly favored by the king because of his grace and intelligence. However, there are some in court who are envious. They tell the king Avenant is bragging that he can bring the princess back. The king puts him in prison for making fun of the king and his ambassador. It happens that the king passes the tower where Avenant is complaining and learns of Avenant's loyalty; so he sends him to bring back the princess. On his way he meets a carp who had jumped too far out of water and could not get back until Avenant helped. The carp thanks him saying, ". . . je vous le revaudrai." Next he saves a crow from an eagle and he replies, ". . . je vous le revaudrai." Thirdly, he saves an owl caught in nets. He, too, replies, ". . . je vous le revaudrai." The princess receives Avenant but will not listen to any marriage proposal until three conditions are made: 1) that he bring her the ring she lost in the river a month ago (the carp helps Avenant get it); 2) that he bring the head of a giant who is ravishing her people (the crow plucks out the giant's eye and permits Avenant to cut off his head); 3) that he bring her marvelous water from the dark cave (the owl goes in the cave and gets it for him). The princess agrees to marry Avenant's king. When she praises him so at court, the envious people there make the king jealous. Again, he locks Avenant in a tower. The princess pleads for him, to no avail. The king decides he isn't handsome enough; so he tries her magic water which the servant has spilled and replaced with a similar phial she had seen in the king's room. It is the poison the king uses to kill princes and lords when they are criminals. At the king's death the queen frees Avenant and offers him her hand and her kingdom.

Moral: Generosity and loyalty bring reward.

3. *L'Oiseau bleu*

A king loses his wife and is inconsolable until a neighboring queen comes, also in mourning, and grieves with him. Soon they are married. Each has a daughter. Her daughter is called Truitonne because she resembles a trout, spotted and slick. His daughter is beautiful and is named Florine. A King Charming comes to court and falls in love with Florine. However, the queen tells him that Florine will not come out until her own daughter is married. He tries to arrange a rendez-vous with Florine, but the queen tricks him by putting Truitonne in Florine's place at her window at night. He puts a ring on her finger and they go to her fairy godmother's castle for the wedding. There, he discovers their ruse. Soussio, the fairy, and Truitonne try to prevail on him to marry Truitonne. When nothing will make him give up Florine, the fairy metamorphoses him into a blue bird for seven years. He flies around the castle and hears Florine's plaints. He tells her who he is and what has happened. He visits her often and brings her gifts. The queen finds the jewels and sends a spy to watch Florine. They learn of the visits of the bluebird and put knives and swords in the cypress near Florine's window. He is wounded. His enchanter rescues him and takes him back to his castle. The enchanter arranges with Soussio to bring Truitonne to his kingdom and return the king to his former self. Soon he will decide to wed her. Meanwhile, Florine begins a search for her bluebird. She meets an old lady who gives her four magic eggs. With the first two she arrives at the palace and with the other two she tricks Truitonne into allowing her to spend the night in the chamber of echoes. There, she reminds the king of their promises, his metamorphosis, etc. He comes to her in the chamber of echoes, and the enchanter and the fairy who gave Florine the magic eggs have united against Soussio. When Truitonne comes to complain, they change her into a trout. The king and Florine make preparations for their wedding.

Moral: Marry for love.

4. *Le Prince Lutin*:

A king and queen have a son who is short as a dwarf, ugly and malicious. His governor has a handsome son, Léandre, who is often mistaken for the prince while Furibon, the king's son, is taken for the court buffoon. Furibon is so jealous that Léandre is sent by his father to a castle he has in the country. One day, Léandre is in the garden and a snake comes up to him while he is playing his flute. She asks him to save her from the gardener who is trying to kill her. He locks her in a room. Furibon comes hunting with his assassins. Léandre saves Furibon from a lion; yet Furibon says he will have him killed if he appears before him again. When Léandre decides to travel, he frees the snake, but to his amazement he finds a lovely lady, "la fée Gentille." She grants him a wish for saving her life, for she lives one hundred years in her fairy form and one week as a snake. She suggests that he become a *lutin* so that he can become invisible and travel easily. She gives him three roses: the first provides him with money; another permits him to know if his mistress is faithful; and the third prevents him from being ill. Léandre first plays a trick on Furibon; then he scares the parents of a young girl so they do not marry her to an old man. He arrives at another court and becomes interested in a young lady, Blondine. He tries his rose on her and it becomes faded so that he knows she is not faithful. He saves a young girl from becoming a vestal virgin and provides her young man with money. His last adventure is to save a young lady, Abricotine, from robbers. Abricotine is the servant to a fairy's daughter. The fairy has had bad experiences with men; so she banishes them from her daughter's kingdom, that is, "l'île des Plaisirs tranquilles." Léandre goes to the kingdom and falls in love with the fairy princess. Furibon is also in love with her from seeing her portrait. Léandre provides anything the princess wishes for. Furibon comes to attack. Léandre pretends to be an Amazon so he can cut off Furibon's head. Finally, "la fée Gentille" persuades the princess' mother that this young man will be true. The wedding takes place for all the nymphs in her kingdom as well as for Léandre and his princess.

Moral: Beware of false love.

5. *La Princesse Printanière*:

The evil fairy Carabosse holds a grudge against the king. His daughter is born and all the good fairies come to endow her with beauty, wit, nice voice and all the virtues. Carabosse gives her "guignon" or bad luck until age twenty. The last fairy lessens Carabosse' curse by granting the daughter a long life of happiness. They put the princess in a tower. When she is a young lady, Fanfarinet arrives to ask for her as Merlin's son's wife. Printanière forces her servants to permit her to watch him arrive. She falls in love with Fanfarinet. A dwarf arrives in behalf of the fairies with gifts: crown, scepter, brocaded dress, skirt of butterfly wings and a box of precious stones. Printanière and Fanfarinet escape to the Desert Isle of Squirrels with the jeweled dagger and crown belonging to her parents. The king is ruined by the wedding. They go after Fanfarinet. On the island Fanfarinet is so hungry that he forgets all about love. The rosebush gives honey to Printanière, but she gives it to Fanfarinet. The oak gives her milk and she gives that to Fanfarinet. Finally the elm gives her "dragées et tartelettes" and tells her not to share with him. Fanfarinet comes to kill her and eat her. She becomes invisible with the aid of a magic stone from the crown. She kills Fanfarinet as an example to faithless lovers. She looks up and sees two chariots combatting in the air. It is Carabosse and the fifth fairy. Carabosse is defeated. Merlin's son arrives, and they don't tell him of the "enlèvement."

Moral: Reason should rule over the heart.

6. *La Princesse Rosette*:

Two brothers have a sister, Rosette. At her birth there is a prophecy that she will cause them misfortune. The king and queen go to an old hermit for advice. He tells them to lock Rosette in a tower. When Rosette is fifteen, the king and queen die. She is freed from the tower. The first thing she sees is a peacock and when she learns it is sometimes eaten, she vows that she will only marry the king of the peacocks. Her brothers set out to find him, worrying all the while about having little peacocks for nephews. The king agrees to wed her if she is as beautiful as her portrait. Otherwise, he will kill her brothers. Because her nurse wants her own daughter to marry the king, they throw Rosette overboard with Frétillon, her dog, who is green and one-eared. Naturally, the nurse's daughter does not resemble the picture, so the king gives the brothers seven days grace. An old man finds Rosette and they are both hungry. She sends her dog to the best kitchen to find them food. The best food being in the king's kitchen, the dog takes it and the king has to go three days without food. At last, the king's confidant follows the dog and finds the old man and Rosette, whom he brings before the king. He learns that she is Rosette. They plan to wed, but not before he pardons the nurse and frees her brothers.

Moral: Clemency, such as that of Louis, is admirable.

7. Le Rameau d'or

King Brun has a humpbacked, cross-eyed little monster for a son, but "jamais une si belle âme n'avait animé un corps si mal fait" (p. 149). They call him Torticoli because everything about him is crooked. The king wants to marry him to Trognon, for she, too, is deformed. The son is not pleased at the prospects of such a bride, so his father puts him in the tower. There, he finds his picture painted on the wall and in a manuscript he observes tiny figures who tell him they will reward him if he returns their queen to them. They also tell him he will have a bad time if he does not. He enters a closet and finds a talking hand. The hand tells him that he can be a big help to him in finding his loved one whose portrait he shows him. He tells him to go into the gallery to the spot where the brightest rays of the sun are. He finds the sleeping beauty. She speaks of her dear Trasimène whose hand has been separated from her. Birds enter and music plays. A large eagle gives him a golden bough with ruby cherries on it. He taps the princess with it. She shouts to the eagle, calling him Trasimène. She tells

Torticoli that she has been enchanted for two hundred years. She grants him a wish. He thinks first of helping her, but she confides that another will take care of her. He then asks to be less ugly. She renders him "Sans-Pair" by three taps with the golden bough. She is the fairy Bénigne. He next finds himself in a forest near the tower. The guards cannot find Torticoli so they tell the king he is sick, then that he died. Trognon arrives and the king blames her for the loss of his son and sends her to the tower. She, too, finds herself depicted in the paintings on the windows. She cries and an old lady appears who is, like Trognon, a legless cripple. She gives Trognon a choice between beauty and virtue. She chooses virtue — an eternal treasure. She follows by chance the same path as Torticoli and finds the hand. The voice tells her to take the hand, hide it in her bed and to give it to the eagle when she sees it. After three days the eagle appears, receives the hand and becomes Trasimène, the young prince enchanted two hundred years ago by an enchanter who was jealous of their love. He grants her a wish. This time she chooses to be beautiful and he names her Brillante and she looks like the shepherdess whom she had admired in the painting. She meets Sans-Pair who wishes to woo her, but she flees him, saying she must obey her *devoir*, not her *passion.* An enchanter falls in love with her and when she will not marry him, he turns her into a grasshopper. An old lady shows Sans-Pair the way to the castle where Brillante is. He finds a large old fairy who wants him to love her. When he refuses, she turns him into a cricket. He calls on the fairy Gentille, who tells him to look for the golden bough. When they find it, they take their former appearance. Bénigne and Trasimène come to inform them that their parents meant them for each other. They are given the palace and the golden bough.

Moral: Elect a beautiful soul in preference to physical beauty, which
    soon fades.

8. *L'Oranger et* l'abeille:

A king and queen only want for one thing — a child. Even though she is old, the queen finally gives birth to a daughter, Aimée. While the nurse has the baby in the sea, a tempest comes up and all perish except the baby in her cradle. She is found by two ogres, Ravagio and his wife Tourmentine. They take her in and do not eat her. After fifteen years the king sends for one of his nephews to take over his throne. On the way, the nephew, Aimé, is shipwrecked on the island where Aimée lives. She hides him in a cavern and brings him food. She gives him her golden chain and her turquoise heart. He knows she is his cousin when he reads what is written on the heart. One day she is stuck by a thorn on returning home and cannot return to the cavern the next day; so he comes to her. The ogre wants to eat Aimé, but Aimée convinces him to save Aimé to eat on her wedding day to one of the ogre's sons. The ogres put a golden crown under their pillows each night, so Aimée takes one of theirs to put under Aimé's pillow. The ogre eats one of his own by mistake. Aimée takes Tourmentine's magic wand and wishes to speak the same language as Aimé. He tells her of her heritage. She makes a cake with a bean in it that continues talking while they escape. Ravagio dons his seven league boots. With the wand, Aimée metamorphoses them: first into a pond, boat and boatman; next into a picture, column and a dwarf and finally into a box, an orange tree and a bee. The bee stings the ogre and some travelers take the wand, so they remain orange tree and bee. Princess Linda comes along and picks an orange. The bee is jealous and stings her. Linda comes and cuts the tree, which bleeds. The bee goes to Arabia to get some magic balm to heal him. Linda is so upset that she calls in some fairies, among them Queen Trusio. She changes them back to Aimée and Aimé. Trusio knows the king, Aimée's father, so she sends them back to him in her flying chariot. They marry and name their first son "Amour fidèle."

Moral: Let reason rule over passion.

9.   *La bonne petite souris*

There is a war between two kings. King Joyeux is killed and the other king takes the queen, who is pregnant, and locks her in a tower. He sends for a fairy to tell him if the child will be a girl or a boy, for if it is a girl, he hopes to marry her to his son. The fairy consoles the queen and tells the king it will be a beautiful girl, Joliette. He gives the queen three peas a day. A little white mouse appears and she shares her peas. Immediately an excellent meal appears. An old lady passes and wants the mouse to eat, but the queen won't permit it. The mouse talks, takes Joliette to care for. Her enemy, Cancaline, steals the child and fifteen years pass. The king's son is going to marry a girl who tends turkeys but who doesn't want to marry him, for he is ugly. They tie her up and take her anyway. The good fairy arrives and the mouse bites the king's ears which bleed and bleed. The mouse also eats the son's only eye, so that the king and his son fall on each other and kill each other. They free Joliette who is locked up with forty keys and hunt for a handsome prince. Joliette loves him and they wed and rule the kingdom happily.

Moral: Show a grateful heart to those who befriend you.

10. *Le Mouton*:

A king has three daughters, but the youngest, Merveilleuse, is his favorite. He goes away to war and returns. He asks each daughter why she is wearing the color dress she wears. He is disappointed that Merveilleuse wears white simply because she looks good in it. He asks them to tell him their dreams. When he hears Merveilleuse tell that she dreamed that he was giving his second daughter in marriage and that he held a golden ewer and was offering to wash Merveilleuse's hands, the king thinks that she wants to dominate, so he has her taken to the forest to be killed. Her monkey, dog and Mooress accompany her. All three offer to have their tongue cut out to be sent back for hers. The monkey's is too small, the Mooress' is too black and the dog's is just right. Merveilleuse meets a sheep with golden horns. The ugly fairy Ragotte had loved him and had turned him into a sheep when he spurned her. He tells her that many of the sheep here were enemies of Ragotte and often leave the flock to return to their former selves. She says she would be less bored here if she could only see her monkey, dog and Mooress. Immediately they are before her. When she learns that her first sister is to be married, she wants to go. He permits it if she will give her word to return. She goes and leaves a box of precious stones. Next, she goes to the second sister's wedding and her father recognizes her and keeps her from leaving. He washes her hands and the dream comes true. While she is recounting all that happened to her, the sheep comes to the palace and asks for her. When the guards refuse to admit him, he dies.

Moral: The highest are subject to the same fortune as the lowest.

11. *Finette Cendron*:

A king and queen are chased from their kingdom and become very poor. Consequently they decide to abandon their three daughters. Fine-Oreille, the youngest, hears their plans and goes to her fairy godmother for advice. Her fairy godmother gives her a ball of yarn so she can find her way back home. The sisters offer to give her a doll if she will lead them back too. However upon returning, they beat her. The second time the mother tries to lose them the godmother gives her a sack of cinders. The third time, they are on their own, for Finette has irritated her godmother by bringing back her sisters the second time. They decide to leave a trail of peas, but the pigeons eat them. They are lost. They find an acorn, plant it and an oak tree grows which they use as a lookout. Finette sees a large palace. It turns out to be an ogre's palace. They all become his prisoners. However, they convince the ogre's wife that they can help her with her housework. Finette tricks the ogre by having him stick his tongue on the stove to see if it is hot enough and she cuts off his wife's head. The sisters take Finette's clothes that her godmother had given her and go to the ball. Finette finds a key in the fireplace which opens a large box of beautiful clothes. She, too, goes to the ball in her red velour mule embroidered with pearls. She leaves without the mule and the prince searches for the one who can wear it, for he hopes to marry her. Finette goes and takes the mate with her, for she suspects that it has something to do with the matter at hand. Prince Chéri gives her parents back their kingdom, since he has a hundred, and weds Finette. She forgives her sisters and they become queens too.

Moral: A magnanimous heart is a just vengeance.

12. *Fortunée*:

A poor laborer dies and leaves a small inheritance to his son and daughter. To his daughter, Fortunée, he leaves a pot of carnations and a ring given him by a great lady. To Bedou, the brother, he leaves stools and a chicken. The brother will not share with his sister. She goes to get some water for her carnations and meets a lady being served a lovely dinner. It is "la Reine des bois" and she invites Fortunée to join her. While she is gone, Bedou steals her carnations, and leaves cabbage in their place. Fortunée gives the ring to "la Reine des bois." When she returns, the cabbage talks — tells her that Bedou took her carnations. She takes his chicken and it talks. The chicken tells her she is the daughter of the queen whose sister was a fairy. The chicken was the laborer's wife changed by the fairy into a chicken because she talked too much. The fairy came a second time and gave the laborer the carnations and the ring. The king's men came after her and she turned them into cabbages like the one she had been talking to. They have not been able to talk until recently. Fortunée goes to get her carnations and finds an army of rats awaiting her. They bite her and the blood flows. She pours water from the golden vase and they flee. She takes her carnations, waters them and they talk in order to admire her. Bedou arrives and puts her out. The "Reine des bois" wants to avenge her, but Fortunée will have no part in it. The carnation becomes a handsome prince, son of the "reine des bois," and is just now disenchanted, for the queen-fairy had foreseen that Fortunée would water the carnations from the golden vase and put the ring on her finger which would ensure their happiness. Fortunée is not sure how she feels about the prince yet, but after forgiving her brother and having the fairy grant him better looks and more wit, she consents to marry Oeillet. The wedding lasts several years.

Moral: Virtue and merit are true *noblesse*.

13. *Babiole*

A queen desires children, but the fairy Fanferluche was angry at her mother when the queen was born and wished her misfortune. A little old lady comes to announce a child who will cause the queen many tears. It is Fanferluche. She gives the queen a white thorn to put on the child's head to protect her from several perils. When she puts the thorn on the child, she becomes a she-monkey. She tells the king that the princess is dead and sends her to be drowned. The valet likes the box she is in, takes her out and sees a chariot drawn by six unicorns; in it are the queen's sister and her four-year-old son. She asks for the monkey as a pet for her son. The queen names her Babiole — plaything. Babiole is dressed like a princess and learns all the proper things a young lady should do. After four years she talks. Her reputation spreads far and wide. The monkey-king, Magot, sends a delegation headed by Mirlifiche to ask her to marry him. Mirlifiche and Gigogna arrive with a parakeet as interpreter. The queen is indebted to Magot, so she tells Babiole she must marry him. Babiole, on the other hand, confesses her love to the prince, but he spurns her. Babiole escapes to avoid marriage to Magotin. She ends up in a cave with an old man. He predicts that the prince will not always be cool toward her. He is Biroqua, father of the river Biroquie. He gives her a turtle to take her where she wants to go. The envoy returning to Magot spots her and captures her. They stop in her mother's kingdom where monkeys have been forbidden since her birth. They are arrested and the guards are impressed with Babiole. The queen sees her and offers her a dwarf as mate. She escapes again, spending the night in an oak tree. She arrives in the desert and is hungry. She eats the olive in her box, sent by Magot earlier, and the box emits a perfume that changes her to her real self. She decides to eat the nut and workmen appear to build a palace. Giants and pygmies come to her court. At a joust she sees her cousin who has come to the court incognito and has learned to love her. She is so disturbed that she goes in the Evil Woods. The fairy Fanferluche is there and takes Babiole up in a black cloud. However, she jumps from the cloud and falls into a bottle where the fairies keep their "ratafia," a liqueur from almonds, which is guarded by six giants or six dragons. The prince recuperates and goes to look for Babiole on his horse Criquetin, the oldest son of Bucéphale, Alexander the Great's horse. The prince arrives at the river Biroquie and meets Biroqua who tells him Babiole is in the bottle guarded by giants and dragons. Biroqua tells him to leave his horse and mount a winged dolphin. He goes as high as the moon and descends to save her with the magic bone "arête enchantée" that Biroqua had given him. They go to Babiole's kingdom where the prince pretends to be a necromancer. He tells the queen that her ugly monkey is now beautiful and that she ought to patch up the differences with her sister by marrying her daughter to her son. The queen promises to do so if she can see her daughter. All come to the wedding including Criquetin and Biroqua in spite of Fanferluche. They live happily ever after.

Moral: Fear gifts from enemies.

14. *Le Nain jaune*:

A queen loses all of her children except one, so she will not correct this last child. The daughter becomes stubborn, proud, disdainful of all. Her mother calls her Toute-Belle. She is loved by many kings and is the subject of all prose and poetry of the time. Yet, she is indifferent to all suitors. Her mother decides to go for advice to the desert fairy, "fée au désert." She knows the fairy is guarded by a lion to whom one must throw a cake of millet flour, candied sugar and crocodile eggs. She rests on the way and the cake is taken. The lions arrive and she has no help. At the right moment the yellow dwarf appears and says he will save her if she will promise to give him her daughter. She promises in order to save herself. He opens up the orange tree and hides the queen. He shows her the house where Toute-Belle will dwell and tend nettles and thistles. The queen awakes in her room and except for a cap and ribbons, she would not know whether it was real or a dream. The queen acts so strangely that the daughter decides to visit the fairy. She, too, stops at the orange tree and her cake is taken. The yellow dwarf appears and tells her she is promised to him. When the lion comes, she promises to wed the yellow dwarf. She faints and wakes in her own room wearing a ring of red hair which she cannot remove. She decides to wed the King of the Gold Mines. On her wedding day an ugly old lady arrives in a cart pulled by two cocks from India. It is the desert fairy. She is accompanied by the yellow dwarf. He claims her since she gave him her word. He fights the King of the Gold Mines amid thunder and lightning. He escapes with Toute-Belle and the desert fairy with the King of the Gold Mines. The desert fairy appears before her king as a nymph, but he recognizes her by her griffin's feet and tricks her into freeing him. As they fly in her chariot pulled by swans, he sees Toute-Belle in the steel house with the sun's rays so hot against it that anyone approaching would be burned. The king pretends to like the desert fairy so that she will permit him to walk along the shore in freedom. He calls on the divinity of the waves and a mermaid comes out of the water holding a mirror in one hand and a comb in the other. She offers to help. She leaves a figure similar to his made of reeds on the beach and takes him to the castle of steel, giving him a magic sword with which to free Toute-Belle. The desert fairy finds the body of reeds and buries it. Meanwhile the king kills four sphinxes, six dragons, twenty-four nymphs. He finds Toute-Belle, falls at her feet dropping the sword. The yellow dwarf grabs it and captures the king. He offers to free him if Toute-Belle will wed him. She will not. The dwarf kills the king and Toute-Belle dies immediately after. The siren or mermaid changes them into palm trees with interlaced branches.

Moral: Do not make a promise unless you can keep it.

15. *Serpentin vert*:

A queen gives birth to twins. She invites all the fairies to come except Magotine. Magotine endows one of the daughters to be the most perfect in ugliness. The other fairies stop her from further mischief and appease the queen by saying that her daughter will be very happy after a certain time. The two daughters are called appropriately Laideronnette and Bellote. Laideronnette asks to become a "solitaire" in order to hide her ugliness. Her parents consent. After two years she returns to Bellote's wedding. They do not want her so she leaves with her servant. One day in the forest she sees a green serpent who tells her that he, too, is unhappy, for he was born handsome. She runs away from him. Later, walking near the beach, she sees a pretty boat and boards it. It sails off and she resigns herself to whatever fate awaits her from Magotine. The green serpent offers to save her life, but she would rather perish than owe her life to him. She wonders at his being able to speak with reason. A voice advises her not to disdain him. Her boat hits a rock and the green serpent saves her. She awakes to find herself not on a rock but in a magnificent palace. It is the land of the "pagodes," little people. Her life there is pleasant, but still there is something lacking. An invisible voice declares his love. She fears it at first. Yet, she becomes bored except in his company. Finally, he tells her that Magotine bewitched him for seven years, two of which are remaining. He asks her to be his wife but to promise not to see him for two years. The "pagodes" tell her the Psyche story. She longs to see her family; so they go for them. After they leave, curiosity overcomes her and she looks at her husband. Magotine arrives with her marionnettes. Polichinelle is her famous general. Magotine makes Laideronnette wear iron shoes which are too narrow. She gives her tasks to perform: to spin spider webs, to make nets; and to remain in chains on a boat. The "fée protectrice" had helped her with the tasks. The green serpent comes to her and they declare their love. Magotine imposes additional tasks: to get water from the source with no end; to climb the mountain with a windmill around her neck to pick a four-leaf clover; and to descend and fill the pierced crock with water of discretion. The protecting fairy helps her again. With two white canaries to lead her, she throws iron shoes at the giants and brings the water back, sprinkles it on Laideronnette, who becomes beautiful. She must spend three years in the woods. Nothing will make her happy until her green serpent is "déserpentiné." At the end of three years she will take the four-leaf clover and the water to Magotine. Because Laideron-nette drank the water and cleansed her soul before her body, the protecting fairy rewards her by shortening her penitence and changing her name to Discrète. In the woods all the animals talk. This is where the fairies put people to do penance. Those who talk too much become parakeets; the gluttons become pigs; the angered become lions, etc. When Discrète returns to Magotine, she demands another task — to go to Proserpine and ask for the essence of life. Her protecting fairy gives her a branch and tells her to strike earth three times while calling on Love. He comes to help her and the green serpent becomes his former self. Love hides in their heart when they go to present the water to Magotine. She even feels its presence, so that she awards them the kingdom of Pagodaland.

Moral: Most of us do not profit from past experiences.

VOLUME II

16. *La Princesse Carpillon*:

A widowed king decides to remarry. His son, Prince Bossu (Humpback), is ambitious and he fears other pretenders to the throne. He consults a fairy and learns that the new queen is already expecting. He decides to play a trick. When the son is born, he has an arrow on his arm. Prince Bossu replaces the child with a cat who bites the queen and causes her to die. Bossu sends the child by a messenger into the forest to be left for the animals to eat. The messenger leaves him with a mother eagle and she raises him with her eaglets. The surrounding country has long been plagued by ogres until the blue centaur saved them from the ogres. However, he demands one child every three years as a sacrifice to him. They find the child the day before their offering is due. They decide to offer this child, but the Amazon fairy arrives to save him by killing the blue centaur. She places the child with an old shepherd called Sublime and his wife. He had three daughters formerly, but lost one when they escaped from a king who had captured them. It was Bossu who had captured them and taken their youngest daughter, Carpillon, as captive because he wanted to marry her. The king protected her until Bossu threatened to dethrone him. Princess Carpillon escapes to become a shepherdess. She aids the Amazon fairy, who then protects her by giving her a bouquet of gilly-flower which makes her unrecognizable to Bossu. The Amazon fairy also sends Carpillon to Sublime. The young prince who is there disguised as a shepherd woos her, but she spurns him because of his low rank. He is wounded saving her from a bear. Finally, she tells the couple her story and they learn that she is their lost daughter. Through the aid of the Amazon fairy they are promised to each other. Carpillon wanders alone into the forest, for she fears her love is condemned. Bossu takes her, but her young shepherd wounds Bossu. The latter plans their death. The Amazon fairy kills Bossu and gives arms to the prince. The king recognizes him as his son and a wedding takes place between equals.

Moral: Love united with reason is glorious.

17. *La Grenouille bienfaisante*:

A king is at war, so he sends his wife, who is pregnant, to a safe castle in the forest. She becomes bored and complains until she has a chariot made so she can go hunting. One day she has a wreck and a gigantic woman in a lion's skin, the fairy lionness, finds her and forces her to accompany her down to the center of the earth, for she is lonely and wants the queen's company. The lionness demands that the queen make a pâté of flies. The queen cannot catch them or cook, so she sits down to bemoan her cruel fate. When she sees a crow about to devour a frog, she gets a stick and makes the crow drop the frog. The frog thanks her and tells

her that all the creatures here were once on a throne or in court.
The frog is half fairy, so she helps the queen make the fly pie. The
second demand of the lionness is a bouquet of rare flowers. The frog
solicits the aid of a bat who flies out to get the flowers. The
frog asks his hood if the queen could escape. It answers that she
must stay and have her child here, that only time can help her.
Meanwhile the king thinks she is dead since he found the broken
chariot. The queen gives birth to a beautiful daughter, Moufette.
After six months the frog offers to go to the king and tell him
she is here. The queen writes to the king with her own blood. It
takes the frog seven years to arrive at the king's palace. The king
is preparing to remarry, but the frog arrives just in time. Everyone is amazed at the frog's performance— changing animals into
flowers, then into a fountain. She gives the king a magic ring to
enable him to see his wife and talk with the lionness. Since the
lionness knows the king is coming, she builds a crystal palace and
puts the queen and Moufette in it. She asks all the monsters who
love Moufette to guard it or lose her. The king fights the lionness
and cuts off her paw. The king tries for three years to reach them,
but the monsters will not let him in. Finally, a dragon agrees to
help if the king promises to give him something to eat of which
he is very fond. The dragon fights the monsters while the king and
others escape. They return to their kingdom and Prince Moufy wins
many jousts and contests in order to please Moufette. She agrees
to marry him. He goes back to his kingdom to prepare for the
wedding. Meanwhile a giant arrives, ambassador to the dragon, and
asks for the king to keep his promise. He learns that the food
craved by the dragon is "Moufette en pâté." The giant offers to
save Moufette if she will wed his own nephew. Moufette remains
faithful to Moufy. They prepare for the sacrifice when the queen
calls on the frog. She gives Prince Moufy a flower that turns into
an extraordinary horse that shoots fire, bombs and bullets. She also
gives him a sword with one diamond. He kills the dragon and a
prince comes out who has been a dragon for sixteen years. The
frog becomes a great queen for the wedding and praises Moufette
for her fidelity — a quality which Mme. d'Aulnoy considered rare
in her day.

Moral: Constant husbands and sincere friends are not of our
century.

18. *La Biche au bois*:

A king and queen are saddened because they have no children. One day she complains by a fountain and a crayfish tells her of a hidden palace where it leads her to have a child. When the crayfish comes out, it is an old lady with grey hair. They take the path of the fairies to the palace of diamonds. The queen doesn't know whether it is real or a dream. Six fairies present her flowers and tell her she will have a beautiful daughter and to name her Désirée ("car il y a longtemps que vous la désirez! "). They also remind her to call them at her birth. The queen returns home, gives birth to Désirée and calls the fairies, but forgets the crayfish. The fairies bring a crib supported by four cupids. If she cries, they rock her and put her to sleep. They endow her with virtues, but the crayfish, fairy of the fountain, brings a curse — if the child sees light before age fifteen, she will repent of it. The other fairies build a palace with an underground entrance with no windows or doors. They also include history on the walls to help the princess learn. They have Désirée's portrait made and it goes everywhere. A young prince falls in love with her portrait, but he is already promised to the Black Princess. He has won three battles so they call him Prince Guerrier. He pleads to wed Désirée. They send Becafique, a young gentleman, to ask for Désirée. The Tulip fairy comes to warn the queen not to let him see Désirée nor to let her leave before she is fifteen. The prince becomes ill when he learns that she will not come. Becafique returns to tell them of the prince's condition. They relent and send Désirée in an enclosed carriage with ladies in waiting, Giroflée and Longue-Epine. The latter, with the mother's help, cuts a hole in the carriage and Désirée sees daylight and becomes a white doe. Longue-Epine then pretends to be the princess and goes to Prince Guerrier, but he calls her a skeleton and locks her and her mother in the château des Trois-Pointes. The prince leaves the court to lead a solitary life with his companion Becafique. The fairy Tulipe leads Giroflée to the forest to keep Désirée company. She also promises Désirée that she will be a doe only in the daylight; at night she will take her own form. Tulipe leads them to an old lady in a cabin and asks her for a room. Prince Guerrier and Becafique come to the same cabin for a room. The prince walks in the forest and sees the doe. He would like to hunt, but not in his weakened condition. He sleeps and she comes to sleep near him, but flees when he awakens. He chases her, catches her and caresses her. However, she escapes when he goes to get her some water. The next day he sees her and shoots her in the leg. He tends her wound and takes her back to the cabin. He ties her to a tree and goes to get Becafique to help. Meanwhile Giroflée finds her and frees her just as the prince returns. Giroflée claims that the doe belonged to her first, and she proves it by having the doe obey her commands. They follow them back to the cabin and Becafique recognizes Giroflée as one of Désirée's ladies. Becafique makes a hole in the partition between their rooms and they overhear Princess Désirée talk of her metamorphosis. The prince goes to her and she never becomes a doe again. The prince's army arrives, for they were going to declare war on Désirée's father for the affront to the prince. While the prince relates all the happenings to his father, Désirée and Giroflée appear well dressed, thanks to Tulipe who is also the old lady of the cabin. Désirée asks forgiveness for Longue-Epine and her mother, and all prepare for the wedding. Becafique even asks his master to arrange for him to marry Giroflée at the same time. Tulipe gives Désirée four gold mines in India so that she will not have less than her husband.

Moral: A young girl should not enter the world too soon.

19. *La Chatte blanche*:

A king has three sons. They are ready to rule the kingdom, but he is not ready to relinquish it to them. He eludes them with different tests. First, he asks them to find a pretty little dog to keep him company in the country. The winner will get the kingdom. They are to return in one year. The brothers leave, swearing friendship forever. The youngest son sets out catching all kinds of dogs, but letting them all go. Nightfall finds him in a thunder storm. He takes the first path toward a light in a castle. There is a golden door with jewels and a porcelain wall. It tells the history of the fairies since creation. It mentions *Peau-d'âne, Finette, Oranger, Belle au bois dormant* and *Prince Lutin,* who was her uncle "à la mode de Bretagne." He pulls the foot of a deer and bells ring, the door opens and he sees a dozen hands holding a torch. Other hands push him through sixty rooms. Finally they dress him elegantly, powder him, coif him and lead him into a room where a history of cats is represented — *Rodilardus, chat botté,* etc. There are two places set and the cat orchestra begins to "miauler." A veiled, small, black figure appears followed by a cortege. She welcomes him. He is astonished that a lovely white cat can speak. She is served rats and mice, but she assures him that his dinner is prepared without them. She has a portrait of him. After supper she entertains him with a ballet by cats dressed as Moors and Chinese. The next morning he is awakened to go on a hunt. He has a wooden horse and she rides a monkey. He expresses the wish that he were a cat or that she were a young lady. She reminds him that he has not found a dog and his year will be up in three days. She tells him the wooden horse will get him there and she gives him an acorn with a small dog inside. On the way he meets his brothers and shows them an old work dog for his choice. They laugh at their young brother. The king is trying to decide between the dogs of the two older brothers when the youngest arrives with his acorn and the dog inside on a piece of cotton. The dog dances the sarabande. The king proffers a second task — they must find a piece of cloth fine enough to pass through a needle's eye. The youngest sets out on his wooden horse to find his white cat. She assures him she will help him with the second task. They are served a "medianoche" and watch fireworks. Another year passes and this time he returns in a carriage with white cats painted all over it. The cloth is in a nut which he must break in the king's presence. The oldest brother has a piece fine enough to go through a large needle, but the youngest breaks the nut and inside is a hazel nut, inside that is a cherry seed, inside that an almond, then a grain of wheat, then a grain of birdseed. He thinks the white cat has made fun of him. He feels a scratch on his hand and it bleeds. Inside the grain of millet is an infinitesimally small cloth depicting all the animals, birds, plants, planets, kings, queens and subjects. It passes through the needle six times. Everyone marvels at the beauty of the cloth. The king presents his third task — to find the most beautiful girl. The son will marry her and they will be crowned king and queen. The youngest returns to the white cat. She promises to help him in this task too. She announces a naval battle between her cats and the rats of the next country as a sort of entertainment for him. He asks her if she is a fairy or if she is metamorphosed. When the time comes to go, she tells him he must cut off her head and tail and throw them into the fire. He cannot do it, but she insists saying that it is the only way he can keep his brothers from winning the throne. When he throws her into the fire, she becomes a beautiful young girl, and all the cats become lords and ladies. She relates her story. She was born a princess, for her father had six kingdoms. When her mother was expecting her, she traveled to a mountain she had heard of. They passed by a fairy castle and the mother entered because she craved their fruit. She pitched a tent and stayed for six weeks. The fairies told her they would give her all the fruit she could carry away if she would give them one gift — her daughter until she marries. The queen agreed in order to save herself and her daughter. The king was furious when he heard what she had done and refused to give them his child. However, they sent a dragon to menace his six kingdoms and he acquiesced. They led her to a mountain in great pomp and the king carried an olive branch to show his submission. The fairies were kind to her. She had a parakeet and a little dog that talked. A young man came by and heard her conversing with them, and became fascinated. She threw him a turquoise ring. The fairies decided to marry her to the fairy king Migonnet who had eagle feet. She resolved to die rather than to marry him, so she went away with her young man. She married him with her dog and parakeet as witnesses. The fairies arrived riding on a dragon that devoured the prince. She jumped in too, but they pulled her out and condemned her to be a white cat until she could be saved by a gentleman resembling her young prince. Before they go before his father for the final test, she resumes the form of a white cat. When the king comes, she turns into a beautiful girl with blond hair. The king awards them the kingdom, but she gives each of the brothers one and they still have three. She becomes known for her kindness, liberalities, merit and beauty.

Moral: Mothers, detest this mother's conduct and do not imitate.

20. *Belle-Belle ou le chevalier Fortuné*:

Two kings are at war. One is defeated, but he doesn't accept it. Rather, he rallies those in his kingdom to help him build an army. Each family is to send one soldier or pay the penalty, a tax. An old gentleman on the border ("de la frontière") is too old to go and too poor to pay the tax. The oldest of his three daughters disguises herself as a male and sets out to fight. On the way she meets an old shepherdess who asks her to help her get her sheep out of the ditch. When she fails to stop, the old lady cries out, "Goodbye, disguised one." Realizing her disguise is lost, she returns home. The second daughter sets out on the same adventure with the same result. The youngest daughter, Belle-Belle, who is her father's favorite, sets out and stops to help the old lady. She is a fairy who rewards her with a horse, Camarade, who will give her advice, for he knows all past, present and future. She also gives her a magic box with twelve changes of clothing and twelve swords. The fairy gives her the name "le chevalier Fortuné." As they go along they meet seven endowed ones: 1) Bucheron, who is strong; 2) Léger, who is quick; 3) Bon Tireur, who sees all; 4) Fine-Oreille, who hears all; 5) l'Impétueux, who can blow as hard as winds; 6) Trinquet, who is a great water drinker; 7) Grugeon, who is a great bread eater. They accompany le chevalier Fortuné and Camarade. Fortuné goes to the king. There, the king and the dowager queen vie for her favor. The queen is attracted to him and the king makes him his squire, instead of sending him to fight. When he spurns the advances of the queen, she lies to the king, saying that Fortuné wants to fight the dragon that has been killing his subjects. Before setting out, Fortuné asks for the king's portrait and infuriates the queen. The seven endowed ones go with him and provide his food. They come to where the dragon is and Fortuné asks his horse's advice. Camarade dreams on it and then tells Fine-Oreille to listen, Trinquet to drink the water from the pond, Forte-Echine to bring wine to fill the pond. The dragon will drink and become drunk. Then Fortuné has only to stab him. He ties the dragon to a special contraption and takes it to the king so he can give it the final blow. The queen cannot endure Fortuné's disdain; so she tells the king Fortuné wants to go recover his lost treasures from the Emperor Matapa. Fortuné asks Matapa for the treasures, not by force, but by remonstrances. The emperor makes conditions: 1) eat all the bread cooked one day for the inhabitants of his city which was larger than Paris, Rome and Constantinople; 2) drink all the water in the city's fountains; 3) run against his daughter. Naturally the endowed ones help him accomplish all the tasks, and the emperor

liberties with one of his rank. He sends her to a cabin with an old lady in it where she can stay if she will say that Constancio, the young prince, sent her. Constancio asks the queen to accept her young shepherdess for the royal flock. Constancio decides to avoid the shepherdess because of his feelings toward her, but he is jealous when he hears her sing of love for a young man as he wanders by. He plants a spy, Mirtain, to watch her and find out her feelings toward the prince. At last, the prince comes to confess his love and she is indignant that he would express such sentiments to a simple shepherdess. He becomes very ill. They ask Constancia to come and cure him with her herbs. However, it is with her glances, not her herbs, that she cures him. She is convinced of his sincerity and confesses her true rank to him. They promise to wed each other. The queen is suspicious and sends the prince to another court while she tries to get rid of the shepherdess. First, she surrounds Constancia by snakes in the garden, but she simply walks through them. Next, she sends her into the perilous forest for a "friendship belt," "ceinture d'amitié," which would have killed her had a fairy not told her how to make the belt harmless. Finally, the queen sends her far away on a ship as a slave. When the prince returns, the queen tells him that Constancia was sick and died. He wants to kill himself, so the queen confesses what she has done. The prince sets out in search of his princess. At the first port he finds thirty giants with one eye each, hammering on an anvil. He inquires about Constancia and they continue hammering until a child comes forth from the fire. It is Cupid. He tells the prince to jump into the fire, but only if his love is pure. He loses consciousness and sleeps thirty hours. Upon awaking he discovers that he is a pigeon and tries to kill himself again, but two girls find him and decide to put him into a torte for the fairy Souveraine. He overhears them talking and learns that Souveraine is on her way to help Constancia who is in a tower, prisoner of a giant. She tells him that she caused his metamorphosis to test his candor. She wants him to take a magic ring and fly to Constancia, put it on her finger and she will become a dove. He does so and they fly off together. They decide to spend the rest of their lives as pigeon and dove, free from duties of courts and free to love each other. They plan to choose a pleasant land and bring Ruson to live with them happily. Cupid and the fairy Souveraine

give their blessings and assure them that if they tire of the metamorphosis, they can return to their original forms.

Moral: When love is pure, all vicissitudes add to the pleasure.

22. *La Princesse Belle-Etoile et le Prince Chéri*:

A princess is poor and widowed with three daughters — Roussette, Brunette and Blondine, the youngest and the prettiest. The
mother cooks and one day an old lady comes to be fed. She cannot
pay, but promises a wish to each. The king comes with his en-
tourage. Blondine wishes to be his wife, Roussette wishes to be
the wife of the admiral and Brunette wishes to be the wife of the
prince, the king's brother. So it happens. When they return to court
with their new wives, the queen mother is furious. When the king's
wife gives birth to three children, the queen mother substitutes
dogs for the children. She has her servant, Feintise, strangle the
king's children and the son of Brunette. Instead, Feintise places
them on a boat in the sea. A privateer and his wife find them and
keep them, for they have stars on their foreheads and jewels fall
when they brush their hair. There is a strong attachment between
Belle-Etoile and Prince Chéri. One day she overhears the privateer
and his wife say that they were not their children and that Prince
Chéri was probably not her brother. They set out to look for their
real parents. They were going to make a sacrifice to the gods and
fairies of a turtledove, but Belle-Etoile saves the bird, which promises to help her in turn. A siren appears and directs them to the
beautiful city where they want to go. The queen mother recognizes
them and tells Feintise to get rid of them. She tempts Belle-Etoile
by telling her of three marvelous objects that will enhance her
beauty: the water which dances, the apple that sings and the green
bird. Chéri obtains the first two easily with the aid of the dove.
For the last task, all three brothers are trapped and enchanted.
Belle-Etoile comes, and with the aid of the dove, saves them all.
Back at the court, the queen mother has persuaded the king to
remarry, but Belle-Etoile and her brothers arrive with the three
magic objects to entertain them. The bird reveals their origin and
the king gives Belle-Etoile to Chéri. The queen mother is put in the
tower; Roussette and Feintise are put in the dungeon with dogs
biting them. The real mother is brought back to the throne. The

old lady at the beginning was the siren and the dove. She brings the privateer and his wife to the wedding too.

Moral: Love is the origin of *gloire*.

23. *Le Prince Marcassin*:

A king and queen are sad because they have no children. One day while picking some flowers, she eats some strawberries and falls into a deep sleep. She dreams that three fairies pass by. The first endows her with a handsome son and the second gives him all the virtues. The third laughs and mumbles something between her teeth. The queen gives birth to a wild boar — Marcassin. The king wants to drown him, but the queen decides to save him and train him to behave as a young prince. The queen is walking one day near the place where she had her dream and wondering why the fairies played this trick on her. An oak pushes out of the ground and a lady appears to her, telling her that one day her son will be all she had hoped for. A lady comes to court with three daughters. The oldest, Ismène, is lovely and sought after at court, especially by Coridon. The king and queen are about to announce the engagement of Ismène and Coridon. Marcassin loves her and pretends a prince would be better suited to her, but she is not ambitious and prefers Coridon. Marcassin goes to the queen and tells her he would like to marry Ismène. His mother says that she is not up to his social level. Marcassin vows he will have her or die. In spite of her love for Coridon, Ismène is made to marry Marcassin. However, on her wedding night Coridon is waiting with a dagger. He kills himself and she kills herself. Marcassin then decides he would like to wed the second sister, Zélonide. The king and queen think he has caused enough trouble, but they finally consent. On the wedding night Zélonide tries to stab him and he jumps on her and kills her in defense. Marcassin decides to leave the court and become a real boar in the forest. In the forest he meets Marthésie, the youngest sister. He asks her to marry him and she consents if he will go back to court. He tricks her into going to his cavern with him and will not let her go. They are wed and she is very considerate of Marcassin. She expects a child. One night she awakens to hear talking and someone leaves the cavern. She goes out and finds a boar skin. Marcassin has been metamorphosed into a handsome man. He tells Marthésie his story about how the third fairy willed that he be a boar until he had married three times and the third wife had found the skin. It was the third fairy who came to harass him every night. There is a tremor and six distaffs appear — three white and three black. A voice tells them they will be happy if they can guess what they represent. Marcassin guesses that the three white ones are the three fairies and Marthésie guesses that the three black ones are her two sisters and Coridon. All return from the other world. They return to court and all are happy to see that the prince looks like his father and that he soon becomes father of a son who bears no resemblance to a boar.

Moral: Better not to know love than not to know wisdom.

24. *Le Dauphin*:

A king and queen have several children, but the youngest, Alidor, is very ugly. The parents are so repulsed by him that he decides to leave. They send after him, but to no avail. Soon they forget him. Along the road Alidor meets a young man who says he is squire to the king of the woods, "Roi des Bois." The young man speaks of the king's daughter, Livorette, and of her beauty. Alidor asks if he would be welcome at the king's court and he assures him he would be. However, Livorette laughs at his ugliness. He admires her although she is rude. They recognize Alidor's noble qualities. One day Alidor goes fishing to try to catch something to please Livorette. He catches a dolphin who pleads with Alidor to free him. Alidor throws him back and wanders off in a dream-like state when the dolphin returns to ask him what he would like in return. Alidor asks for the best fish in the sea. The dolphin tells him he will always be ready to help him. Alidor asks that the Princess Livorette love him or that he die. The dolphin turns Alidor into a canary, but he can become himself at any time. He flies up to Livorette's balcony and she is charmed by him. She calls him Biby and keeps him in the room with her other animals. He asks the king and queen if he can marry Livorette. They consent if Livorette will agree. They all laugh about her canary-husband. He demands to stay in her room and does. She falls into a deep sleep and Alidor comes to her. The next day Alidor goes to thank the dolphin and he sits on a rock where an old lady comes out. It is

Grognon who says she does not like him. The dolphin tells him that she will try to prevent him from helping Alidor. The king and queen seriously consider marrying Livorette to a handsome prince. Alidor wants to declare himself as her husband, but when he reminds her that she is already married, they laugh. Livorette falls ill and the doctor tells her she is pregnant. The king wants to throw her and the monkey-monster she gives birth to off a precipice, but the queen intervenes. The princess is locked in a tower and Alidor is so grieved that he throws away all he has and is left in rags. The child is allowed to live only so the king may learn who the father is. He holds an audience so that all the court can bring the child a present. The king observes everyone to see if the child caresses one more than the others. Alidor is made to come and he picks up a pin on the way as a gift for the child. The child jumps on him and kisses him. The king puts all three of them on a raft with milk, wine and bread. Alidor, who is half crazy by now, eats all the bread and drinks all the wine. He calls on the dolphin who comes and he wishes for music. Livorette says his wishes are useless, that he should let her make the wishes. She asks that they be taken to a beautiful island and have a beautiful palace with a river of wine and a river of water. She asks who was the father of her child and the dolphin replies that it was the canary, Alidor. She then asks that the dolphin make Alidor sane again. She is pleased to hear the dolphin tell of Alidor's noble birth. They thank the dolphin and reign as king and queen of the island. Alidor wants to celebrate their marriage, but Livorette says she will never consent without her parents' permission. The king is distraught at what he has done so they go to the fairy Grognette who tells them to go to the Dolphin Island. They are in a tempest and wreck. The dolphin carries them to the island, but after six years all are changed. They tell of their cruelty to Livorette and they all weep together. They accuse the king and queen of taking some precious jewels, but it is a trick to prove Livorette's innocence. She says she is innocent as they are and asks forgiveness. They are wed. Their life is as long and happy as it had been sad and upset at first. They return to their own kingdom and their son remains on Dolphin Island.

Moral: The richest treasure is a faithful friend.

25. *Le Prince Adolphe et la Princesse Félicité*

ou

L'Ile de la Félicité

A young prince in Russia who makes war and hunts bear becomes lost one day when a storm comes up in a forest. He sees a light and climbs a nearby precipice and enters a cavern. There, he finds an old lady. She tells him that he is the first mortal she has ever seen in this place. It is the home of Eole, god of the winds. Eole is gone with his children to do good and evil in the world. Soon they return. There is the west wind, the northeast wind, the southwest wind, Eole, Borée, and several "Aquillons." They talk to the Prince Adolphe, but their breath is so cold it freezes him. They brag of their exploits. Finally, the mother misses Brother Zéphire. Then Adolphe sees a young man as handsome as Cupid appear. Zéphire is late because he had been in Princesse Félicité's gardens caressing her with his balmy winds. Adolphe becomes interested and asks where she reigns. Zéphire answers that it is "l'île de la Félicité." Many people seek the island, but "Envie" chases them away. Adolphe spends the night with Zéphire and questions him at length about the Princesse Félicité. Adolphe longs to see her. Zéphire agrees to take him on his wings and gives him a green coat which will make him invisible. Adolphe wakes Zéphire as soon as Aurore appears. Zéphire confesses that he is in love with a rose in the garden. As they approach the island, Adolphe worries that he might not speak the same language as Félicité, but Zéphire assures him that Félicité's is universal and they will soon speak the same language.

The fairy palace is made of diamonds and other precious jewels. Adolphe admires the gardens with the statues of Love. He falls asleep there, but wakes to search for an entrance to the palace. He sees a maiden lower a basket for a gardener to fill with flowers for the princess. Adolphe, still with his invisible coat, jumps into the basket. He admires the palace and follows the nymphs in to see the princess. He reveals himself to her and they fall in love. One day Adolphe worries about being away from his kingdom for as long as three months. She tells him he has been there three hundred years! He thinks that his kingdom will now be in other hands and he regrets that the mores and customs will be so strange to him now. He is ashamed to have spent so much time with his mistress. He is concerned about his "vertu" and his "gloire." Adolphe plans to leave the island in order to perform some action that will make him wòrthy of her. She gives him arms and a magnificent horse, Bichar, who will lead him to a worthy deed. She warns Adolphe not to put his foot on the ground until he reaches his own country. Otherwise, Bichar will be unable to help him. She provides all this through her gift of magic. He is so eager to go that he forgets his green coat. As they are climbing a narrow path, their way is blocked by a cart filled with wings. An old man asks for help and Adolphe puts his foot on the ground to help him. The old man is "le Tems" and he covers Adolphe's mouth and stifles him. Zéphire is passing by at this moment and he tries to revive Adolphe, but to no avail. He carries him back to the island, puts him in a cave and covers him with flowers. He also engraves a verse:

> Le tems est le Maître de tout ...
> Qu'il ne se trouve point d'éternelles Amours,
> Ni de Félicité parfaite.

The princess finds him and grieves ever after. She shuts the gates of the palace and no one has been received since. Men should realize

> Que le temps vient à bout de tout,
> Et qu'il n'est point de félicité parfaite.

> *Moral*:   Time is the master of all.
> There is no perfect happiness.

BIBLIOGRAPHY

Arzelier, F. Martin. *La Mythologie et la théologie des contes d'enfants.* Neu-
chatel: J. Sandoz, 1871.

Aulnoy, Comtesse d'. *La Cour et la ville de Madrid vers la fin du XVIIe siècle,
Relation du Voyage d'Espagne.* Paris: Plon, 1874.

————. *Les Contes des fées.* 2 vols. Paris: Mercure de France, 1956.

————. *The Ingenious and Diverting Letters of the Lady: Travels into Spain.*
London: C. P. Putnam, 1899.

————. *Les Contes des fées ou les Fées à la mode.* Tome Premier, avec une
préface par M. de Lescure. Paris: Librairie des Bibliophiles, 1881.

Aurevilly, J. Barbey d'. *Femmes et moralistes.* Paris: Lemerre, 1906.

Barchilon, Jacques and Henry Pettit. *The Authentic Mother Goose Fairy Tales
and Nursery Rhymes.* Denver: Alan Swallow, 1960.

Baring-Gould, Sabine. *Curious Myths of the Middle Ages.* Boston: Roberts
Brothers, 1868.

Bédier, Joseph. *Les Fabliaux, Etudes de littérature populaire et d'histoire littéraire du Moyen Age.* 4e ed. Paris: Champion, 1925.

Beeler, James R. "Madame d'Aulnoy, Historical Novelist of the Late Seventeenth Century." Unpublished dissertation, University of North Carolina
at Chapel Hill, 1964.

Bernard, Catherine and Charles Perrault. *Les Deux Riquet à la Houppe.* Paris:
La Centaine, 1929.

Bernard, Catherine. *Inès de Cordoue, Nouvelle Espagnole.* Vol. I of *Bibliothèque de Campagne ou Amusemens de l'Esprit et du Cœur.* 12 vols. La
Haye: Jean Neaulme, 1753.

————. *Eleonore d'Yvrée ou les Malheurs de l'Amour.* Vol. VI of *Bibliothèque de Campagne ou Amusemens de l'Esprit et du Cœur.* 12 vols. La
Haye: Jean Neaulme, 1753.

————. *Histoire de la Rupture d'Abenamar et de Fatime.* Vol. I of *Bibliothèque de Campagne ou Amusemens de l'Esprit et du Cœur.* 12 vols. La
Haye: Jean Neaulme, 1753.

Borgerhoff, E. B. O. *The Freedom of French Classicism.* New York: Russell
and Russell, 1968.

Boussel, Patrice, ed. *Histoires et Légendes de la Normandie mysterieuse.* Paris:
Tchou, 1970.

Brochon, Pierre. *Le Livre de colportage depuis le XVIe siècle, sa littérature
et ses lecteurs.* Paris: Librairie Gründ, 1954.

Buchan, John. "The Novel and the Fairy Tale," *The English Association,*
No. 79 (July, 1931), 3-17.

Bulfinch, Thomas. *The Age of Fable or the Beauties of Mythology*. New York: The Heritage Press, 1942.

Cherbuliez, Victor. *L'Idéal romanesque en France de 1610 à 1816*. Paris: Hachette, 1911.

Chujoy, Anatole and P. W. Manchester, eds. añd compilers. *The Dance Encyclopedia*. New York: Simon and Schuster, 1967.

Cirlot, J. E. *A Dictionary of Symbols*. Translated by Jack Sage. New York: Philosophical Library, 1962.

Clouston, W. A. *Popular Tales and Fictions, Their Migrations and Transformations*. Vol. I. London: William Blackwood and Sons, 1887.

Cumings, Edith K. "The Literary Development of the Romantic Fairy Tale." Unpublished dissertation, Bryn Mawr, 1934.

Dallas, Dorothy. *Le Roman Français de 1660 à 1680*. Paris: Gamber, 1932.

Danois, Countess. *The Lady's Travels into Spain or a Genuine Relation of the Religion, Laws, Commerce, Customs, and Manners of that Country*. London: T. Davies, 1774.

Delaporte, P. V. *Du Merveilleux dans la littérature française sous le règne de Louis XIV*. Réimpression de l'édition de Paris, 1891. Genève: Slatkine Reprints, 1968.

Delarue, Paul. *Le Conte populaire français*, Vol. I. Paris: Editions Erasme, 1957.

――――. *Le Conte populaire français*, Vol. II. Paris: Editions Erasme, 1965.

Deloffre, Frederic. *La Nouvelle en France à l'Age Classique*. Paris: Didier, 1967.

Desplantes, F. and P. Pouthier. *Les Femmes de Lettres en France*. Réimpression de l'édition de Rouen, 1890. Genève: Slatkine Reprints, 1970.

Deulin, Charles. *Les Contes de ma mère l'oye avant Perrault*. Réimpression de l'édition de Paris, 1879. Genève: Slatkine Reprints, 1969.

Dévigne, Roger. *Le Légendaire des provinces françaises à travers notre folklore*. Paris: Horizons de France, 1950.

Dictionnaire de Biographie française, sous la direction de J. Balteau, M. Barroux, et M. Prevost. Paris: Letouzey et Ané, 1933.

Diderot, Denis. *Entretien entre Diderot et d'Alembert, La Rêve de d'Alembert, Suite de l'entretien*. Paris: Garnier-Flammarion, 1965.

Dontenville, Henry. *La France mythologique*. Paris: Tchou, 1966.

Dunlop, John. *The History of Fiction*: Being a Critical Account of the most celebrated Prose Works of Fiction from the Earliest Greek Romances to the novels of the present age. 4th ed. London: Reeves and Turner, 1876.

Edmonson, Munro S. *Lore, An Introduction to the Science of Folklore and Literature*. New York: Holt, Rinehart and Winston, 1971.

Evans-Wentz, W. Y. *The Fairy Faith in Celtic Countries*. New Hyde Park, New York: University Books Inc., 1966.

Félice, Ariane de. *Contes de Haute-Bretagne*. Paris: Editions Erasme, 1954.

Fénélon, François de Salignac de La Mothe. "De l'éducation des filles," *Œuvres*. Tome XVII. Paris: J. A. Lebel, 1823.

Foulché-Delbosc, R. "Madame d'Aulnoy et l'Espagne." Madame d'Aulnoy, *Relation du Voyage d'Espagne*. Paris: Klincksieck, 1926.

Fowlie, Wallace. *Love in Literature: Studies in Symbolic Expression*. Bloomington: Indiana University Press, 1965.

――――. *The French Critic 1549-1967*. Carbondale and Edwardsville: Southern Illinois University Press, 1966.

France, Anatole. *Le Livre de mon ami.* Ed. by J. Heywood Thomas. Oxford: Basil Blackwell, 1957.

French Books: A Comprehensive Selection. New York: French Book Corporation of America, 1973.

Fromm, Erich. *The Forgotten Language, An Introduction to the Understanding of Dreams, Fairy Tales and Myths.* New York: Rinehart and Co., 1951.

Godenne, René. *Histoire de la Nouvelle Française aux XVIIᵉ et XVIIIᵉ siècles.* Genève: Librairie Droz, 1970.

Green, Frederick C. *French Novelists, Manners and Ideas from the Renaissance to the Revolution.* New York: D. Appleton, 1929.

Gregory, Horace, ed. *Ovid The Metamorphoses.* New York: The Viking Press, 1958.

Hartland, Edwin Sidney. *The Science of Fairy Tales, An Inquiry into Fairy Mythology.* New York: Frederic A. Sockes Company, 1890.

Hazard, Paul. *Les Livres, les enfants et les hommes.* Paris: Hatier, 1967.

Heuscher, Julius E. *A Psychiatric Study of Fairy Tales: Their Origin, Meaning and Usefulness.* Springfield: Chas. C. Thomas, 1963.

Hubert, Renée. "L'Amour et la Féerie chez Madame d'Aulnoy," *Romanische Forschungen,* 75 (1963), 1-10.

———. "Le Sens du voyage dans quelques contes de Madame d'Aulnoy," *French Review,* Vol. XLVI, No. 5 (April, 1973), 931-37.

———. "Poetic Humor in Madame d'Aulnoy's Fairy Tales," *L'Esprit Créateur,* III, No. 3 (1963), 123-29.

Jal, Auguste. *Dictionnaire critique de biographie et d'histoire.* 2ᵉ éd. Paris: Henri Plon, 1872.

Jones, Shirley. "Examples of Sensibility in the Late Seventeenth Century Feminine Novel in France," *Modern Language Review,* LXI (April, 1966), 208.

Jung, C. G. *The Archetypes and the Collective Unconscious. The Collected Works of C. G. Jung.* Translated by R. F. C. Hull. Vol. IX, Part 1. London: Kegan Paul, 1959.

Kready, Laura. *A Study of Fairy Tales.* New York: Houghton Mifflin, 1916.

Krüger, Kurt. *Die Märchen der Baronin Aulnoy.* Inaugural Dissertation. Leipzig, 1914.

La Fayette, Mme. de. *Isabelle ou le journal amoreux d'Espagne.* Paris: Pauvert, 1961.

La Fontaine, Jean de. *Les Fables* présenté par Jean Giraudoux. Paris: Gallimard, 1964.

———. *Œuvres complètes.* Présentation et notes de Jean Marmier. Paris: Editions du Seuil, 1965.

La Force, Mlle. de. *Gustave Vasa, Histoire de Suede.* Vol. I of *Bibliothèque de Campagne.* 12 vols. La Haye: Jean Neaulme, 1753.

———. *Histoire secrette des amours de Henry IV, Roi de Castille.* Vol. III of *Bibliothèque de Campagne.* 12 vols. La Haye: Jean Neaulme, 1753.

Lang, Andrew. *Adventures among Books.* New York: Longmans, Green, 1912.

———. *Myth, Ritual and Religion.* Vol. II. New York: Longmans, Green, 1906.

Lescure, M. de. "Mme d'Aulnoy et les contes de fées au XVIIᵉ siècle," in *Les Contes des fées de Mme d'Aulnoy.* Tome premier. Bibliothèque des dames. Paris: Librairie des Bibliophiles, 1881.

Lewis, C. S. *Of Other Worlds, Essays and Stories.* Ed. by Walter Hooper. New York: Harcourt, Brace and World, 1966.

Linker, Robert White, ed. *The Lays of Marie de France.* Chapel Hill: University of North Carolina, 1947.

Loeffler-Delachaux, M. *Le Symbolisme des contes de fées.* Paris: Editions du Mont-Blance et l'Arche, 1949.

Lüthi, Max. *Once Upon a Time On the Nature of Fairy Tales.* Translated by Lee Chadeayne and Paul Gottwald. New York: Frederick Ungar, 1970.

Massignon, Geneviève, ed. *Folktales of France. Folktales of the World Series.* Ed. by Richard M. Dorson. Chicago: University of Chicago Press, 1968.

Merla, Patrick. " 'What is Real?' Asked the Rabbit One Day," *Saturday Review — The Arts* (November, 1972), 43-50.

Mongrédien, Georges. *La Vie quotidienne sous Louis XIV.* Paris: Hachette, 1948.

Montégut, Emile. "Des Fées et de leur littérature en France," *Revue des deux mondes* (1er avril, 1862), 648-75.

Morrissette, Bruce Archer. *The Life and Works of Marie-Catherine Desjardins* (Mme de Villedieu) *1632-1683.* New Series, Language and Literature, No. 17. Saint Louis: Washington University Press, 1947.

Palmer, Melvin D. "Madame d'Aulnoy and Cervantes," *Romance Notes,* XI (1970), 595-98.

Pilon, Edmond, ed. *Mme d'Aulnoy — Mme de Murat — Mlle de la Force — Mlle Lhéritier de Villandon — Mme Pauline de Beaumont: Bonnes Fées d'antan.* Paris: E. Santot et Cie., 1909.

———. *Muses et Bourgeoises de jadis.* Paris: Editions Excelsior, 1933.

Propp, V—. *Morphology of the Folktale.* Translated by Laurence Scott. Bloomington: University of Indiana Press, 1958.

Rat, Maurice. *Aventurières et Intrigantes du Grand Siècle.* Paris: Librairie Plon, n.d.

Ravenel, Florence Leftwich. *Women and the French Tradition.* New York: Macmillan, 1918.

Reynier, Gustave. *La Femme au XVIIe siècle.* Paris: Tallandier, 1929.

Roche-Mazon, Jeanne. *Autour des contes de fées,* Recueil d'études de Jeanne Roche-Mazon. Paris: Didier, 1968.

Rougemont, Denis de. *Love in the Western World.* New York: Fawcett World Library, 1956.

Sorel, Charles. *La Bibliothèque Françoise de M. C. Sorel.* Paris: Par la Compagnie des Libraires du Palais, 1664.

Soriano, Marc. *Les Contes de Perrault, Culture savante et traditions populaires.* Paris: Editions Gallimard, 1968.

Storer, Mary E. *Un Episode littéraire de la fin du XVIIe siècle La Mode des contes de fées.* Paris: Champion, 1928.

Thompson, Stith. *Motif-Index to Folk-Literature*: A Classification of narrative elements in folk tales, ballads, myths. 6 vols. Bloomington: University of Indiana Press, 1955.

———. "Narrative Motif-Analysis as a Folklore Method," *FF Communications,* LXIV (July, 1955), 3-9.

———. *The Folktale.* New York: The Dryden Press, 1946.

Tolkien, J. R. R. *Tree and Leaf.* Boston: Houghton Mifflin, 1965.

van Gennep, Arnold. *La Formation des legendes.* Paris: Flammarion, 1912.

———. *Manuel de Folklore français contemporain.* Tome Premier. Paris: Editions Auguste Picard, 1943.

Villars, Montfaucon de. *Le Comte de Gabalis ou entretien sur les sciences secrètes.* Paris: A. C. Mizet, 1963.

Villedieu, Madame de. *Les Désordres de l'amour*. Edition critique de M. Cuénin. Genève: Librairie Droz, 1970.

Walckenaer, C. A. "Lettres sur les contes de fées attribués à Perrault et sur l'origine des fées," in *Mémoires, Contes et Autres Œuvres de Charles Perrault*. Paris: Librairie de Charles Gosselin, 1842.

Yearsley, Macleod. *The Folklore of Fairy-Tale*. London: Watts and Company, 1924.